The Congo

WORLD BIBLIOGRAPHICAL SERIES

General Editors:
Robert G. Neville (Executive Editor)
John J. Horton

Robert A. Myers   Ian Wallace
Hans H. Wellisch   Ralph Lee Woodward, Jr.

John J. Horton is Deputy Librarian of the University of Bradford and currently Chairman of its Academic Board of Studies in Social Sciences. He has maintained a longstanding interest in the discipline of area studies and its associated bibliographical problems, with special reference to European Studies. In particular he has published in the field of Icelandic and of Yugoslav studies, including the two relevant volumes in the World Bibliographical Series.

Robert A. Myers is Associate Professor of Anthropology in the Division of Social Sciences and Director of Study Abroad Programs at Alfred University, Alfred, New York. He has studied post-colonial island nations of the Caribbean and has spent two years in Nigeria on a Fulbright Lectureship. His interests include international public health, historical anthropology and developing societies. In addition to *Amerindians of the Lesser Antilles: a bibliography* (1981), *A Resource Guide to Dominica, 1493-1986* (1987) and numerous articles, he has compiled the World Bibliographical Series volumes on *Dominica* (1987), *Nigeria* (1989) and *Ghana* (1991).

Ian Wallace is Professor of German at the University of Bath. A graduate of Oxford in French and German, he also studied in Tübingen, Heidelberg and Lausanne before taking teaching posts at universities in the USA, Scotland and England. He specializes in contemporary German affairs, especially literature and culture, on which he has published numerous articles and books. In 1979 he founded the journal *GDR Monitor*, which he continues to edit under its new title *German Monitor*.

Hans H. Wellisch is Professor emeritus at the College of Library and Information Services, University of Maryland. He was President of the American Society of Indexers and was a member of the International Federation for Documentation. He is the author of numerous articles and several books on indexing and abstracting, and has published *The Conversion of Scripts, Indexing and Abstracting: an International Bibliography* and *Indexing from A to Z*. He also contributes frequently to *Journal of the American Society for Information Science, The Indexer* and other professional journals.

Ralph Lee Woodward, Jr. is Director of Graduate Studies at Tulane University, New Orleans, where he has been Professor of History since 1970. He is the author of *Central America, a Nation Divided*, 2nd ed. (1985), as well as several monographs and more than sixty scholarly articles on modern Latin America. He has also compiled volumes in the World Bibliographical Series on *Belize* (1980), *Nicaragua* (1983), and *El Salvador* (1988). Dr. Woodward edited the Central American section of the *Research Guide to Central America and the Caribbean* (1985) and is currently editor of the Central American history section of the *Handbook of Latin American Studies*.

VOLUME 162

The Congo

Randall Fegley

Compiler

CLIO PRESS

OXFORD, ENGLAND · SANTA BARBARA, CALIFORNIA
DENVER, COLORADO

British Library Cataloguing in Publication Data

Congo. – (World bibliographical series; vol. 162)
I. Fegley, Randall   II. Series
016.96724

ISBN 1–85109–199–8

Clio Press Ltd.,
55 St. Thomas' Street,
Oxford OX1 1JG, England.

ABC-CLIO,
130 Cremona Drive,
Santa Barbara,
CA 93116, USA.

Designed by Bernard Crossland.
Typeset by Columns Design and Production Services Ltd, Reading, England.
Printed and bound in Great Britain by
Bookcraft (Bath) Ltd., Midsomer Norton

THE WORLD BIBLIOGRAPHICAL SERIES

This series, which is principally designed for the English speaker, will eventually cover every country (and many of the world's principal regions), each in a separate volume comprising annotated entries on works dealing with its history, geography, economy and politics; and with its people, their culture, customs, religion and social organization. Attention will also be paid to current living conditions – housing, education, newspapers, clothing, etc.– that are all too often ignored in standard bibliographies; and to those particular aspects relevant to individual countries. Each volume seeks to achieve, by use of careful selectivity and critical assessment of the literature, an expression of the country and an appreciation of its nature and national aspirations, to guide the reader towards an understanding of its importance. The keynote of the series is to provide, in a uniform format, an interpretation of each country that will express its culture, its place in the world, and the qualities and background that make it unique. The views expressed in individual volumes, however, are not necessarily those of the publisher.

VOLUMES IN THE SERIES

Contents

Contents

Contents

Preface

In the course of writing this bibliography, it became abundantly clear that an enormous amount of confusion exists over the Congo. Few people in the English-speaking world realize that a country named the Congo still exists. When speaking of the Congo, it is frequently assumed that one means the former Belgian Congo, now named Zaïre. Indeed in the course of compiling this work, I have noticed that major American and British university libraries and data bases have catalogued information specific to the country under Zaïre. This in itself presents a major barrier to the study of the Congo, formerly the French or Moyen Congo and part of former French Equatorial Africa. Long overshadowed by its giant neighbour Zaïre, the underpopulated and impoverished Congo has seen more than two decades of anti-Western regimes, during which the country's orientation was almost exclusively towards its former colonial master France and the communist world. For these reasons, the Congo is virtually unknown to most of the Anglophone world.

The general aim of this bibliography is to present the Congo in its many facets to the English-speaking world. Items in this work have been selected for their importance, authority, variety and accessibility. Priority has been given to sources in English. However, numerous important French-language works have also been included due to the scarcity of material in English.

Another consideration in choosing entries was the importance of certain fields. Important research in history, demography, ethnology, linguistics, religion and sociology has been conducted in the country. Hence, these areas have a relatively large number of entries. In addition to these, the Congolese and those studying their country have also stressed certain subjects, and these chapters have also been lengthened. These include politics, economics and literature. Recent works in some key fields have been included for their value as updates for other material. Finally, a comprehensive reference to the

Congo could not be compiled without numerous sources from surrounding countries. Hence throughout this work, various sources relating to Zaïre, Gabon, Central African Republic and Cameroon have been included where they also apply to the Congo, particularly in cases where literature specific to the Congo has been scant.

The citation order within each section is alphabetical by author and, in the case of periodicals, by the name of the publication. Items are annotated to provide a summary of each work's contents and other details, such as author, significance and viewpoint. An index of authors, titles and subjects is also included.

I would like to extend my appreciation to the many people who have helped me in this study. I would also like to thank the library staffs at Pennsylvania State University's Berks and Schuylkill Campuses and Harrisburg Area Community College's Lebanon Campus for their assistance. My wonderful wife Connie and boys Ken and Andrew have once again given me their support and assistance.

Randall Fegley
Reading, Pennsylvania
March 1993

Introduction

A Varied Land

Covering an area of 342,000 square kilometres (132,012 square miles), the People's Republic of the Congo (sometimes called Congo-Brazzaville) straddles the equator between 4°N and 5°S in west central Africa, and extends more than 1,280 kilometres (800 miles) inland from the Atlantic Ocean. With a maximum length of 1,006 kilometres (625 miles) and width of 225 kilometres (140 miles), it has a coastline of 150 kilometres (93 miles) on the Atlantic Ocean. It is bordered on the north by Cameroon and the Central African Republic, on the west by Gabon, and on the east and south by Zaïre. The Angolan enclave of Cabinda and the Atlantic Ocean are to the southwest.

The Congo is comprised of four topographical regions: a coastal plain stretching inland about 64 kilometres (40 miles); the Mayombe mountains and the fertile Niari and Kouilou valleys in the south central area; the central Bateke Plateau separating the basins of the Ogooue and Congo rivers; and the Congo River basin in the north, composed of mainly impassable flood plains in the lower portion, and savanna in the upper.

The alluvial coastal zone, running southeast to northwest, is bordered by a sandy littoral plain, about 50 by 40 kilometres (19 by 15 miles). Two spurs of the Mayombe Escarpment, which lie to the east of this plain, emerge on the coast at Pointe Noire and Pointe Indienne. The coastal plain, at its northern end, terminates at the Gabonese Massif. The Atlantic coast of the Congo is washed by the cool Benguela current, and there are many mangrove-fringed lagoons blocked by sand spits, similar to those in the Ivory Coast and Benin. Because of the cool current, temperatures are relatively low, and in places the coastal plain resembles a treeless steppe.

Inland, and parallel to the coast, lies the Mayombe Escarpment, covered by moist forest and segmented by many rivers. Part of the Coast-Congo divide, it rises to between 490 and 800 metres (1,600 and 2,625 feet) and culminates in the Chaillu Massif to the north and the Bateke Plateau to the east, between which lie the valleys of the Kouilou and Niari. These valleys are prolonged on their eastern edge by the Cataractes Plateau, which descends gradually to the Congo River, where it forms cliffs on both banks and rapids in its bed. This divide and its accompanying valleys are crossed by the Congo-Ócean Railway from Pointe Noire to Brazzaville, opened in 1934 to provide a French counterpart to the Belgian Matadi-Kinshasa (Leopoldville) railroad, which was first opened 1898 and later rebuilt. Both of these lines are spectacular feats of engineering, and on the 320 miles of the Congo-Ócean Railway there are no fewer than ninety-two bridges and twelve tunnels, the latter being otherwise almost unknown in tropical Africa. The Niari Basin, like the Ngounie Valley farther north in Gabon, has been carved out of the valley's soft Karoo sandstone. This area, and all of the southeast of the country, has fertile soil and woodland-savanna vegetation. The basin has good economic potential, all the more so because it is served by the railway.

Violent rapids make the Congo river (called the Zaïre in Angola and Zaïre) unnavigable from Brazzaville to the Atlantic. To the east of the capital, the river widens into Stanley Pool, which is fifteen miles across and dotted with many small islands. From Brazzaville inland, it becomes navigable for 1,000 miles. The Stanley Pool region has many bare hills. The savanna-covered Bateke Plateau, extending north of Brazzaville and the Pool, has an average altitude of 600 to 700 metres, and is cut by dry valleys. These are poor, level and separated from each other by the deeper forested valleys of northern tributaries of the Congo.

Farther to the north lies the huge Congo Basin, of which the portion in the Congo Republic is demarcated by a line running from the mouth of the Lobaye to Ouesso, Makoua, Owando (formerly Fort Rousset), Gamboma and Mpouya. This region has the purest type of equatorial climate, while the greatest seasonality and least rainfall are found in the Bateke Plateau. Dry seasons are like those of the southern hemisphere. The Sangha and other rivers to the north flood widely, and there are vast expanses of rain forest and swamp vegetation around them.

The Congo's typically tropical climate has two dry and two wet seasons, which are more clearly marked in the north than in the south of the country. At Brazzaville in the extreme southeast, the longer dry season, characterized by dust, overcast skies and cool weather, runs from mid-May to the end of September. The lesser dry season extends for about one month beginning in late December. The heavy rains occur between late January and mid-May, and the smaller rainy season lasts from early October to mid-December. Humidity is usually high in most parts of the Congo and temperatures average 24°C (75°F) throughout the year. Along the coast the climate is more temperate.

About a quarter of the Congo's area is covered by swamps, nearly half by equatorial rain forest and most of the rest by grasslands. Between the Oubangui and the Likouala, the swamp area includes forest galleries along the river banks, separated by wide stretches of prairie. Trees dot the savanna areas of the south but not those of the sandy Bateke Plateau. The densest forest is dispersed between the Mayombe Escarpment, the Chaillu Massif, and the northwestern area of the Sangha region. In the more accessible areas, intensive felling of the most valuable species has given rise to a secondary forest of pines and bushes.

A Divided People with Lively Cultures

An estimated 2,300,000 Congolese inhabit 342,000 square kilometres of land, an average density of less than seven per square kilometre. One of the region's enduring economic difficulties is the fact that under-population has denied the Congo and its northern neighbours a sufficient labour force. Although the south has significant population clusters, the northern and northeastern savanna, swamp and rain forest are very sparsely inhabited. Almost two-thirds of the population live in Brazzaville, Pointe-Noire, and along the connecting rail line. Outside the main towns, the Congolese are divided into small communities which have little external contact.

The three principal ethnic groups, among some seventy-five distinct subdivisions, are the Bakongo, the Bateke, and the M'Boshi.

Some four million Bakongo inhabit both sides of the river, a quarter of whom are in the Congo and the rest in Angola and Zaïre, where they are the largest single ethnic group. In the Congo they comprise about forty-five per cent of the population and include the Lari and related groups living in the area around Brazzaville and the Vili, a coastal group predominant in the Pointe-Noire area. Most of them are farmers, raising traditional food crops such as cassava, bananas, oil palms, sweet potatoes and maize. Coffee, cocoa and oil palm products are also produced for cash and export. Increasing numbers of Bakongo now live and work in large towns.

The Kongo language, Kikongo, spoken in western Zaïre, northern Angola, and the southern part of the Central African Republic as well as in the Congo, is a Bantu language. It is a tonal language, and nouns are grouped into classes. There are several different local dialects, such as Zombo, Ntandu, Vili and Yombe. A form of Kikongo called Kituba is widely used in west central Africa as a trade language. The oral literature of the Kongo is rich in *ngenda*, praise poems for clans (groups related through descent). Like a number of other languages in western equatorial Africa, Kikongo has an unusual number of words for philosophical and psychological ideas. Children are trained in the art of formal public speaking (*kimphovi*) which is used in legal argument.

Religious movements which combined Christianity with traditional religion have grown up among the Bakongo. In the late 19th century, 'Kimbanguism' developed as an early form of resistance to Belgian imperialism and spread to the Congo, then under French rule. After 1950, the cultural and political *Association des Bakongo* (ABAKO) helped prepare the way for Zaïrean independence. Similar organizations developed in the Congo.

The half-million strong Bateke, spread over a large area north and northeast of the capital, are the most traditional of the ethnic groups, engaging in farming, hunting and fishing. They form about twenty-six per cent of the country's population. Colonialism disrupted the Bateke severely by concentrating wealth in a tiny section of the community, inflating marriage payments, drafting labourers and displacing the tribe from its strongholds around Stanley Pool.

Approximately sixteen per cent of the Congo's population consists of northern Boulangui groups, the most important of which is the M'Boshi. The M'Boshi number some 200,000 people inhabiting the northern part of the country, although a considerable number have migrated to Brazzaville. The Likoula and the Kouyou are the most important M'Boshi sub-groups. The M'Boshi-Kouyou have been active in the Congo's military forces and have dominated its officer corps at times.

The remainder of the Congolese population is made up of various groups shared with Gabon, including the Fang and Bakota. In some areas of the north, small bands of Babinga Pygmies still maintain a nomadic lifestyle, while between 12,000 and 15,000 Babinga have settled in or around northern towns. Several thousand workers from neighbouring African countries have also settled in the Congo, where their welcome has not been warm in recent years. The European community in the Congo has fluctuated widely. The French (perhaps as many as 10,000) have always been the majority of the immigrant group. Russians, Americans, Cubans, Chinese, Japanese, Italians and other Europeans form or have formed small communities.

Tribalism has been one of the enduring, and unfortunate,

characteristics of Congolese life. Rooted in disputed pre-colonial trading rights, inter-ethnic rivalries have pervaded all public life in the country. Since independence, tribal considerations have continued to be extremely important, in spite of the ideological rhetoric of many Congolese leaders and writers.

Cursed though the country may be by ethnic diversity, Congolese culture has been colourful and active. Traditional crafts, such as mask-making and sculpting, have produced many masterpieces. Painting, drawing and other European arts have also had an impact. However, it has been in the field of literature that the Congolese have been most prolific. Numerous works, ranging from poetry to drama to short stories have been produced by Congolese writers such as Sylvain Bemba, Guy Menga and Tchicaya U Tam'si. Politics, particularly those of the left, have been a continuing theme of the country's literature. One unusual aspect of the literary scene in Brazzaville has been the large number of writer-politicians who have emerged, as well as a significant number of politicians who have dabbled in literature.

Religion has also played an influential role in Congolese life, but again ethnicity has been an important consideration in spiritual matters. Animistic worship is still prevalent in the Congo, although most of the urban population is Christian. During the late 1980s approximately fifty-four per cent of the population were Roman Catholics and twenty-four per cent Protestants. However, the most important religions are those ethnic politico-religious cults established by messianic prophets in the first half of the twentieth century. These syncretic sects, which combine traditional and Christian beliefs, include groups founded by Simon Kimbangu, André Matswa, Simon Mpadi and Zephyrin Lassy. Many of their adherents also claim membership in other Christian denominations. More conventional Catholics and Protestants have active churches, missions and other facilities thoughout the country. Virtually all Muslims, totalling less than two per cent of the population, are non-Congolese.

The Economy: Successes, Failures and Potential

The Congolese economy is hampered by difficult terrain and climate; by poor natural resources; and by the country's small population and market, but because of its vital role in transit has been fairly well equipped. The Congo's location at the crossroads of transit trade to and from Zaïre, the Central African Republic, Chad, and Gabon, and the lingering effects of Brazzaville's former position as administrative capital of French Equatorial Africa, have a substantial positive impact on the country's economy. Customs receipts provided twenty-three per cent of government revenue in 1987 and extensive employment in service and transport industries is evidence of the substantial benefits of the Congo's location.

Brazzaville, which contains one-seventh of the country's population, was formerly the capital of French Equatorial Africa and is now the centre of some common services of the four successor states to that French colony: Gabon, the Central African Republic, Chad and the Congo. Of these four, the Congo alone has control over a railway and waterway vital to the other three. Most of the right-bank tributaries of the Ubangi and Congo are navigable. Roads link the railway, navigable rivers and adjacent states, especially the road from Dolisie to Libreville (Gabon) and Cameroon. Brazzaville is a rail-river trans-shipment point on Stanley Pool opposite Kinshasa, Zaïre and, like it, has a good airport. In a survey of ninety-seven cities in 1991 Brazzaville was rated as the world's fourth most expensive city for foreigners to live in. Tokyo, Osaka and Libreville preceded the Congolese capital in this dubious distinction.

The port of Pointe Noire is served by the 610 kilometre Congo-Ócean Railway, connecting it to Brazzaville and the Congo river transport to the north. An eighty-eight kilometre (fifty-three mile) realignment, financed by a multi-donor consortium and the Congolese government and designated to circumvent the most difficult part of the Mayombe Escarpment, was opened in August 1985. Pointe Noire also serves as the port of shipment for large manganese mining operations in Gabon known as Comilog. Ore transport is provided by a 285 kilometre rail link with Mbinda on the Gabonese/ Congolese border. In 1989 Congolese railways carried 434 million passenger-kilometres and 1,037 million tonnes of freight. A two train head-on collision, killing at least 100 people, on 6 September 1991 has brought increased emphasis on safety. Pointe-Noire is also the coastal terminus and port for other Gabonese ores, Congolese timber, and Central African and Chadian cotton and groundnuts, as well as lesser exports and imports. The port's quays are being extended and the town has timber and other works.

International airlines provide services to the Congo, and the government-owned national airline, Lina Congo, provides a domestic air service. The road network is inadequate, making retail distribution in the interior difficult and costly, impeding marketing of rural agricultural products, and limiting the accessibility of rich timber stands in the north.

The Niari Basin is the scene of varied agricultural experiment, public and private, mechanized and traditional, plantation and non-plantation, African and European, pastoral and arable. In the late

1950s a high dam was planned on the Kouilou at Sounda gorge, some fifty miles long, stretching in a straight line from the coast. In general conception akin to the Konkoure (Guinea) and Volta (Ghana) schemes, it would likewise create a vast lake which could be used to evacuate Gabonese timber. More power would be produced than at Kariba, and could supply an industrial complex at Pointe Noire using Gabonese manganese. However, this project is questionable ecologically and has persistently failed to attract enough investment to be realized.

The most valuable mineral is off-shore petroleum, which is now the major source of revenue. Production began in 1978 and rapidly accelerated. Two US petroleum companies, Amoco and Conoco, and European consortiums led by Elf and Agip are currently involved in off-shore production and exploration. Small amounts of oil are produced onshore just north of Pointe Noire, where there is a refinery. Petroleum reserves are estimated to be between 500 and 1,000 million tonnes.

Lead is mined at Mfouati, about half way along the Congo-Ócean Railway. A mine that had been producing 390,000 metric tons of high-grade potash annually at Holle, near Pointe Noire, was flooded in 1977. The geological structure of the ore body has made reopening the mine difficult. US and French firms have undertaken feasibility studies of the possibility of renewing potash exploitation at the flooded site or elsewhere, but it seems unlikely that the operation will be resumed. Gold mining yielded 800 kilograms of refined metal in 1989, as opposed to 5 kilograms in 1985. Copper, zinc, bauxite, iron and phosphates are also found in small to medium quantities.

Timber, which used to be the main export, comes from the Mayombe and Sangha regions, especially from near Ouesso. Limba, mahogany, sapele and okoume are the main species marketed. Two and a quarter million cubic metres of timber were produced in 1983.

Only about fifty per cent of the population is active in the monetized economic sector. Students and other minors account for twenty-five per cent, and the remainder are subsistence farmers or are inactive. Although most people live by farming, this contributes little to revenue and only modestly to exports. Subsistence and export crops are those typical of equatorial regions. Of those involved in the cash economy, ninety-five per cent are engaged in commerce, industry, or with the government; agriculture accounts for only five per cent. The contribution of agriculture to the gross domestic product fell from 6.6 per cent to 6 per cent in 1984. About twenty-seven per cent of the total population is engaged in subsistence farming. Cash crops, none of which are grown in great quantity, include palm kernels, sugarcane, bananas, groundnuts, tobacco, coffee, and cocoa beans. Until recently, most marketing activities for these products were controlled by state boards which have now been abolished. Palm oil and kernels are produced, mostly from plantations, for thirty large processing mills. Some distribution monopolies remain for major commodities, such as sugar and rice. Apart from those related to petroleum and the transport system, the country has only light industries, located mainly in Brazzaville and Pointe Noire. These include wood processing, soap, sugar, palm oil, beer, cement, textiles, and cigarettes. Around 30,000 tonnes of fish are caught annually.

France continues to be the Congo's main supplier of aid as well as its principal trading partner, although since independence trade and aid patterns have shifted somewhat, with the Federal Republic of Germany, the United States, Italy and Brazil increasing their commercial and development involvement. The Congo also concluded several trade agreements with China, the Soviet Union, and other former communist-bloc countries. The Congo, Cameroon, the Central African Republic, and Gabon formed the Central African Customs and Economic Union, to which others have joined since. The Congo also belongs to the Communauté Financiere Africaine and its currency is the CFA franc.

The major emphasis of the government's 1982-86 five-year plan was on infrastructure and other long-term projects. Many projects either were not finished or were suffering from declining revenues and increasing debt service. In June 1985, the Congo instituted a structural adjustment programme designed to re-balance the budget and boost non-oil sector productivity. However, declining oil prices, coupled with the deterioration of the dollar, thwarted full execution of the plan. In 1986, the IMF loan and two French commercial bank loans were needed to make up the shortfall. Nonetheless, major economic imbalance still persisted, and the Congo was forced to slash its 1987 budget projections by fifty per cent. In addition, the country adopted the painful step of reducing public employment, using a combination of attrition and abandonment of the former policy of providing government employment to all university graduates. In compliance with IMF and World Bank requirements, public investment has been scaled down, the country has launched a programme of revitalizing the forestry and agriculture sectors, and several parastatals have been either abolished or given decreased responsibilities.

In recent years, the Congo's economy has been heavily dependent on petroleum earnings, external borrowing and imported goods, including ninety per cent of all meat consumed. Faced with the collapse of world oil prices after 1985 and saddled with a very large foreign debt, the Congo has been under pressure from international lending institutions to implement structural adjustment measures and free-market economic policies. Terms of trade deteriorated between 1985 and 1987. The trade imbalance during that period was US$173 million and represented a decrease of 38.7 per cent in real domestic gross revenue. However, by 1989 exports topped US$1.1 billion (US$916 million of which was petroleum related), while imports were only valued at US$617 million. The Congo's economic difficulties have continued to serve as a driving force behind political reforms.

Early History

Little is known about prehistoric Congo. Although evidence of early habitation has been found near both Brazzaville and Pointe Noire and in the Niari valley, it relates to only about a tenth of the Congo's total area and is so heterogeneous as to preclude any accurate classification concerning age and origin. Scholars believe that the groups now populating the Congo may have found on arriving there a country almost empty of inhabitants except for a few bands of migratory Babinga pygmies. Such information as exists about the Bakongo indicates that they slowly moved south and west from the Chad basin, but did not reach the coast until the early 15th century. Even less is known about the origins of the Bateke, Bakota and Fang. When Europeans first heard of their existence, the Bateke reportedly lived in a huge area extending from the Mayombe foothills to the plateau north of Brazzaville, were organized into a centralized kingdom headed by the *Makoko*, or king, and mined ores at Boko-Sangho and Mindouli.

Recorded history begins with the Portuguese exploration of the coast. In 1484, Diego Cao discovered the mouth of the great river known successively as the Congo and the Zaïre. At that time, the largest concentration of Bakongo inhabited what is now northern Angola, where they had founded their capital, Mbanza-Congo, later renamed San Salvador by the Portuguese. Parts of the Congo, Zaïre and Angola were within the Kongo state which reached its climax in the sixteenth century. Some African leaders in the three modern nations of the Bakongo region aim to reconstitute that ancient state.

The Bakongo had one of the most powerful early kingdoms in central Africa. They had established the kingdom of Kongo south of the lower Congo (Zaïre) River by 1300, and by the 16th century they established vassal states, Loango, Ngoyo and Kakongo, north of the river. The king of Kongo, the *manicongo* was a powerful ruler, who appointed provincial governors in his kingdom. The Bakongo had a well-organized trading system, using palm cloth as money in the north and east, and shells called *zimbu* in the west.

During the 16th century Portuguese missionaries built churches and schools. The *manicongo* Mbembe-a-Nzing (Alfonso I), who ruled from 1506 to 1543, became a Christian, and some Kongo people travelled to Europe. First treating the Bakongo as an equal sovereign power, the Portuguese then became active in the slave trade and this encouraged civil wars which weakened the Kongo kingdom by the mid-17th century.

Among the Kongo groups that migrated from Mbanza-Congo were the Vili. They crossed the Congo River and progressively occupied all the coast as far as Cape Sainte Catherine. The Vili kingdom of Loango, divided into seven provinces, was under the suzerainty of a paramount chief or *Ma Loango*. It reached its climax at the end of the 17th century, when its port had become a major slaving centre, attracting Portuguese, Dutch, English and French traders. Since 1564, Loango had also been the site of a bishopric, from which Catholic missionaries ventured out to evangelize the peoples of nearby regions. Loango grew rich from the slave trade, but in turn it also declined during the 19th century, by which time Portuguese missionary activity had ceased and Roman Catholicism had all but disappeared.

Gradually, under the impact of migrations from Gabon, the Loango kingdom lost its northern provinces, while to the east, the *Makoko*'s Bateke kingdom was being restricted to the Bateke Plateau by the encroachments of the Bakongo from the south and of the M'bochi from the north. Latecomers to the northern region, the M'bochi did not spread fully throughout the Likouala-Mossaka basin until the end of the 18th century. Although the *Makoko* lost control of some land and tribes to the M'bochi, he barred their southward march and the Bateke retained their monopoly of the trade between the north and Stanley Pool. By the mid-19th century, despite continuing internal migrations, the Congo's main ethnic groups were inhabiting much the same areas in which they live today.

French Colonial Rule

The abolition of the slave trade, and the founding of Libreville in 1849 by the French as a haven for freed slaves, gave France an incentive and a base for exploring the interior of western equatorial Africa. No European had penetrated the country which is now the Congo Republic beyond the Mayombe until 1875, when Count Pierre Savorgnan de Brazza started out from Libreville on the first of his three explorations. Pierre Savorgnan de Brazza (1852-1905), a French explorer of Italian parentage, established French influence over what is now the Congo Republic. On his first journey (1875-85), de Brazza travelled up the Ogooue River and into the Congo River Basin. In 1879-82, he travelled up the Congo River and signed a treaty with the *Makoko* of the Bateke. This treaty put land north of the Congo under French protection, ceded to France the site of what became the town of Brazzaville and prevented the Belgian government, which was colonizing the rest of the Congo region through the work of H. M. Stanley, from spreading its control northwards. On de Brazza's third expedition, in 1883, he joined forces with his lieutenant, Albert Dolisie, who had been making treaties with tribes of the lower Ubangui, and together they went on to explore the country as far as the west coast. There de Brazza made a similar protectorate treaty with the Ma Loango, who ceded outright to France the area known as Pointe Indienne.

De Brazza later became Commissioner General for the French colonial government. Always working for good relationships and understanding with Africans, he was known to tell Europeans in Africa: 'Do not forget that you are the intruder who was not invited!' Brazzaville was named after him and African respect for him continues to be apparent in the fact that the Congolese have chosen not to 'Africanize' the name of their capital, in spite of the trend to do so elsewhere on the continent.

Because central Africa had lost much of its interest for European traders after slavery was abolished and the Suez Canal opened, the imperial powers agreed to a negotiated settlement of their competing claims in the region. By the Act of Berlin in 1885, France lost direct access to the mouth of the Congo River, but retained possession of the Niari basin and the lands explored by de Brazza. All the signatory nations agreed to internationalize trade and shipping in the Congo basin and to confirm their respective zones of influence in the hinterland by effective occupation. This Act was supplemented by a series of bilateral treaties demarcating the new frontiers. In 1885 the boundary between the Congo and Cabinda was established by a treaty with Portugal, and an agreement with Germany laid down the frontier with Cameroon; in 1887, two other treaties recognized the Oubangui-Congo rivers as the boundary between the French and Belgian territories. Successive administrative reorganizations of the colony moved control of the southwestern areas from the Ministry of the Navy to that of the Colonies, and united them in a single colony called the Congo Français (French Congo) or the Moyen Congo.

Between 1906 and 1910, all of France's possessions in central Africa were again reorganized as the French Equatorial African Federation which comprised the four colonies of the Moyen-Congo,

Gabon, Oubangui-Chari and Chad. Until French Equatorial Africa broke up in 1959, the Congo was its political and economic core. Brazzaville became the capital of both the Moyen Congo and the Federation, which was headed by a governor-general appointed by and responsible to the French government and Parliament. Theoretically, each of the colonies retained economic and administrative autonomy, but power became increasingly centralized. Ruling by decree and disposing of funds granted by France for the entire territory, the governors-general were able to carry out programmes to develop education, health services, courts and public works on a federation-wide basis, with little control from distant Paris or effective opposition from the territorial governors. In the process, the Moyen Congo received the most-favoured colony treatment. It was provided with the only railroad and deep-water port in all the Federation, and Brazzaville's public buildings, schools, law courts, trading houses, telecommunications and medical services soon surpassed all others. The Moyen Congo's pre-eminence, having been in large part achieved with manpower and funds supplied by the other colonies, caused resentment among its neighbours, especially the older colony of Gabon.

Two offshoots of the Act of Berlin that notably influenced the Moyen Congo's development were the facilities provided for missionary enterprises of all kinds and for concessionary companies. Catholic missionaries, who were the first to evangelize and educate the Congolese, soon encountered competition from Protestants and opposition from socio-political protest movements in the form of messianic cults. The concessionary companies' regime was established by France in 1899, partly to circumvent the principle of economic nondiscrimination among the nations signing the Berlin Act and partly to counter similar measures which had been taken east of the river in the Belgian Congo. By enabling French concessionaries to exploit what were then thought to be the great riches of the Congo, France could avoid international censure, acquire large profits, and economize on the cost of administering huge trackless areas. Some forty companies were granted thirty-year monopolies on the economic production and administration of 650,000 square kilometres in the Congo basin.

The consequences of this system were disastrous in financial and human terms. Ivory and rubber virtually disappeared from the conceded zones. The population dropped by as much as sixty-three per cent in some areas of French Equatorial Africa. Among the primary causes of this decline was the recruitment of porters and forced labour for the building of the Congo-Ócean Railway. The construction of the railway was a scandal in its day. When the figures were finally compared, one African had died for every cross-tie and one European for every kilometre. Imported disease, spread by the new transport system, also took a high toll. Epidemics of smallpox in 1905, Spanish flu in 1918 and venereal diseases throughout the 1920s killed thousands. The French government lost more money than it gained in rents and taxes and French public opinion was shocked by reports of the abuses to which the system had given rise. These reports were largely the work of British author, Edmund Morel, whose Congo Reform Movement was also responsible for uncovering the even more atrocious concessionary system in the neighbouring Belgian Congo. By 1930 most of the companies had gone bankrupt and the system was effectively liquidated.

The situation in the French Congo also deteriorated in 1911 when Germany obtained 107,000 square miles (280,000 square kilometres) of French Equatorial Africa in return for recognition of French dominance in Morocco. The provisions of this agreement gave Germany access to both the Congo and Ubangi rivers by ceding to the German colony Kamerun the Woleu Ntem province of Gabon and two projecting arms of territory which cut Chad and Ubangi-Chari off from Gabon and the French Congo. This disruption of French colonial designs caused much resentment in both Paris and Brazzaville. In the Congo itself, it resulted in the Sangha valley being turned over to Berlin. Following the defeat of the Germans in Kamerun in 1916-17, the territory and rights given to Germany in 1911 were returned to the French. Under the African provisions of the Treaty of Versailles, Kamerun became a League of Nations mandate, partly under the British but mostly controlled by the French, whose dominance in western equatorial Africa was now assured.

The First World War and the economic difficulties of the 1930s fueled African desires for independence. The most important African movement of the pre-Second World War Congo was a social association founded in 1927 by André Matswa, a former Roman Catholic catechist. The movement, called the Association of Natives of French Equatorial Africa (Amicale des Originaires de l'Afrique Equatoriale Française), began in Paris as a type of mutual aid society for French Equatorial Africans who were living in metropolitan France. Stressing education, co-operation and the elevation of Africans to equal status with French citizens, the Amicale movement spread to the colony where it gained wide attention among the Bakongo and their Sundi and Lari subgroups. These groups and Matswa's movement in general were also influenced by the example of the messianic leader Simon Kimbangu in the Belgian Congo. In the Brazzaville area the movement took on strong political overtones that brought about repressive measures by the French authorities. Eventually, Matswa and other leaders were arrested and placed on trial. The decision of the administration, on 3 April 1930, to deport Matswa to Chad incited a series of riots and workers in Brazzaville went on strike. The exile of Matswa and the resulting alienation of the Lari peoples from the colonial authorities had important effects on later political developments. Several Amicale leaders were executed in 1940, and Matswa died in prison in 1942. Rather than destroying the movement, the exile and death of Matswa made him the centre of religious mysticism, similar to that accorded Kimbangu. Large numbers of the Lari would eventually come to believe that Matswa was in Paris negotiating with General Charles de Gaulle and would return as a saviour to liberate them from French rule.

From War to Independence in Two Decades

The Second World War rapidly transformed French Equatorial Africa from one of the most politically and economically under-developed parts of the French Empire into Free France's stronghold in sub-Saharan Africa. Much of the credit for this transformation can be given to a single prodigious individual: Félix Eboué. Born in French Guiana in 1884, he was descended from Africans who had been taken to South America as slaves. He was educated in France and joined the government service as a colonial administrator in French Equatorial Africa. In 1939, at the beginning of the Second World War, Eboué was Governor of Oubangui-Chari, the first man of African descent to become a colonial governor. During the war in Europe, France was occupied by Germany. But in August 1940 Eboué decided to support the Free French Army of General Charles de Gaulle, at a time when most French colonies were backing the Vichy regime. The Moyen-Congo joined Oubangui-Chari and Chad in rallying to General de Gaulle, who appointed Eboué governor-general of French Equatorial Africa. The men and materials that the colonies provided were of great importance in winning the war against Germany. The Moyen Congo's main contribution to the Allied war effort was as a base and transit area. Pointe Noire and the Congo-Ócean railroad operated at capacity to provision troops and ship out French Equatorial Africa's produce.

In spite of all these efforts, the war was not easy for the colonies. It was particularly harsh on the Sara tribesmen of Chad who joined the French Army during both world wars. In North Africa, Indochina and Europe the conditions of service were so bad that more deaths occurred in transit than on the battlefield. Due to these conditions and imported disease, the current population of Chad is less than that before the French presence and its demographic structure has been severely distorted. In the last census, which was concluded in 1965, the sex ratio had just reached forty-seven per cent male to fifty-three per cent female.

Although he served the French empire, Eboué always believed in the value of African cultural traditions and worked to increase African political influence in the French colonies. The Federation emerged from the war with its economy and means of communication greatly improved, its indigenous institutions such as the chieftaincy and customary courts strengthened, and with new municipal governments. These and other reforms introduced by Eboué influenced the recommendations made by the Free French conference which he organized at Brazzaville early in 1944, and many of them were incorporated into the constitution of the Fourth French Republic. When Eboué died in 1944 he was buried in the Pantheon in Paris, an honour which is given only to the greatest heroes of France.

Continuing Eboué's legacy, legislation in 1945-46 abolished forced labour, proclaimed freedom of meeting and association, gave jurisdiction over all penal cases to courts applying French law, laid the legal foundations for extending France's post-war Plan for Modernization and Equipment to the overseas territories, and introduced elective institutions at three levels.

Under the 1946 French constitution, the Moyen Congo's restricted electorate, voting as separate colleges of European and African citizens, chose four representatives to the three parliamentary bodies of France, five to the Grand Council of French Equatorial Africa, and thirty to its own territorial assembly. The so-called political parties organized during the postwar decade were in reality weakly organized tribal and regional groupings, whose strength fluctuated with the internal and external support given to their leaders. In the elections held between 1946 and 1956, most of the Lari refused to participate, because they believed that their dead leader, André Matswa, would return to restore their freedom and ascendancy over the other Congolese tribes. The Lari's abstention left the field open to competition between two tribal parties of approximately equal strength. These were Félix Tchicaya's Parti Progressiste Congolais (PPC), formed by the Vili of the Pointe Noire area, and Jacques Opangault's Mouvement Socialiste Africain (MSA), composed of the northern M'bochi tribes. The support given to Tchicaya by the powerful Rassemblement Démocratique Africain (RDA) and Tchicaya's position as the Moyen Congo's representative to the French National Assembly more than offset help given to Opangault by the French Socialist party. Hence the PPC had a slight edge over its rival.

Ten years later, The Moyen Congo progressed further towards autonomy as a result of the *Loi-Cadre* (Enabling Act) of June 23, 1956. This law eliminated the dual-college system and the federal government-general, enlarged the electorate to comprise all adult Congolese, and augmented the territorial assembly's economic and fiscal powers to include a share in the executive authority. That same year, a Lari priest, the Abbé Fulbert Youlou, convinced his fellow tribesmen that he was Matswa's heir and won their votes for his new party, the Union Démocratique pour la Défense des Interêts Africains or the UDDIA. After being stripped of his priestly duties by his superiors who charged him with indiscipline, lack of zeal and neglect of his pastoral duties in favour of politics, Youlou was elected mayor of Brazzaville in November 1956. While the politics of tribalism were played out, a forty-five-man assembly elected on 15 May 1957 chose from its ranks the members of a new government council, *Conseil de Gouvernement*, whose vice president Jacques Opangault became prime minister of the Moyen Congo in all but name.

In 1958 General de Gaulle's return to power in France accelerated the Congo's political evolution. He proposed holding a referendum on the constitution of the Fifth French Republic, in which France's overseas dependencies were to choose between maintaining colonial status, gaining full independence without further French aid, or becoming members of a federal Franco-African community of autonomous republics. On his tour of the African territories a month before the referendum of September 1958, de Gaulle selected Brazzaville as the site for his important announcement that states which voted to join the Community could later opt for independence if they so desired. On September 28, the Moyen Congo registered the highest proportion of affirmative votes (339,436) to negative ones (2,122) in French Equatorial Africa. Two months later its assembly voted to join the French Community as the autonomous Congo Republic. On 8 December 1958 Abbé Fulbert Youlou was invested by the assembly as prime minister and head of government. Riots in Brazzaville in February 1959 led to the arrest of Opangault, whose political influence was severely reduced. Tchicaya's following had also dwindled with his increased involvement with affairs in Paris rather than at home. New National Assembly elections were conducted on 14 June 1959 and Youlou was elected President of the Republic on 21 November of that same year. It had taken four years, marked by inter-tribal strife, for Youlou to eliminate his rivals by force or by persuasion and to rise to the presidency. In the process, he overtly favoured his fellow tribesmen, neglected economic issues, became absorbed in unrealistic and unpopular foreign ventures, alienated his Francophone African neighbours and was increasingly obsessed by his fear of Russian and Chinese Communism.

Meanwhile on August 15, 1960, the Congo took the final step of proclaiming its independence, after signing agreements for defence and co-operation with France and for the co-ordination of economic, financial and cultural measures with the other French Equatorial African states. On September 20, 1960, the Congo Republic was admitted to membership in the United Nations. The span of fourteen years in which the Congo moved from the status of a colony without any elective bodies to that of a sovereign nation was too short for the development of more than nominally democratic institutions. Ethnic conflicts, labour shortages and a lack of university-educated professionals would be continuing difficulties which would make themselves felt quickly.

Revolution and Reality in the Congo

Youlou's blatantly unfair ethnic politics united his tribal and ideological opponents against him. Tensions increased in August 1963 with a draft scheme to merge opposition parties into a one-party system and to make the trade unions government-directed. During this month, when thousands of university and high school students were on holiday, mass demonstrations in Brazzaville were incited by the trade unions. Large numbers of unemployed also became involved in the protests. The arrest of trade union leaders on August 13 provoked a general strike in Brazzaville, Pointe-Noire and Dolisie (now Loubomo) during which the arrested trade unionists were freed by force. The government proclaimed a state of emergency, but after secret deals President Youlou resigned on August 15 and the army agreed to maintain order while a provisional government was being formed. With the army's support, a coalition of non-Lari leaders set up a Conseil National de la Revolution (CNR) headed by Alphonse Massamba-Débat, a Bateke Socialist and former minister. The French government did not intervene, either to support Youlou or to recognize his successor officially, until 8 December 1963, when by a massive vote the Congolese approved Massamba-Débat's constitution and elected a new National Assembly. Eleven days later Massamba-Débat was elected president of the republic and on Christmas Eve 1963 the formation of the first government of the second Congo Republic was announced. The three days of August 13 to 15 which brought about the fall of the Youlou regime, became known as the *Trois Glorieuses*, or three glorious days, and are celebrated every year.

The 1963 Constitution, a presidential-parliamentary arrangement like that of France, established a two-man executive, the president of the Republic and the prime minister. The new president, Alphonse Massamba-Débat, was a political figure, unlike the prime minister, Pascal Lissouba, who was a doctor of science and an agricultural expert. This government was evidence of the first major departure from colonial policy in central Africa and of an increasingly marked swing towards revolutionary leftism. In January 1964 the Congo recognized the People's Republic of China. Later that year the Mouvement National de la Revolution (MNR) was formed as the only legal political party, declaring itself for Marxism-Leninism, anti-colonialism and non-capitalist development. Its youth wing, the Jeunesse du Mouvement National de la Revolution (JMNR), developed into a para-military force and wielded increasing power. State planning was introduced with the first Five-Year Plan (1964-1968) and a state sector was built up in industry, trade and agriculture. On 1 April 1965 former president Youlou was able to escape to Léopoldville (now Kinshasa) in the former Belgian Congo. He went on to Spain were he died in exile on 6 May 1972.

A new pattern of political conflict emerged from 1963 to 1968. On the one hand was the growth in influence and power of the MNR, both as a political machine and as a socialist vanguard spawning a militant Cuban-trained 'civil defence' movement and the JMNR's 'people's militia'. On the other hand, the army, an essentially conservative force drawn into constant conflict with the JMNR, was undergoing its own more limited radicalization. In managing these disparate political forces, Massamba-Débat, who remained as president throughout this period, was at first carried by the momentum of the party's growth. His moves to control the party in 1967 and 1968 came too late and by July 1968 he was in open conflict with both the party and the army. It was through these developments that Captain Marien Ngouabi, a charismatic young paratroop officer, emerged as a figure powerful enough to maintain the delicate balance between army and party that was to characterize political life for nearly a decade after Massamba-Débat's fall from power.

On 8 January 1966, the MNR had been declared the 'supreme organ of the nation'. Conflict between government and party caused Lissouba to resign as prime minister in April. On May 6 Massamba-Débat agreed to let the party nominate Ambroise Noumazalay to lead a new government. There were then attempts by the army to curb the MNR. In violent incidents in June 1966 the army hierarchy moved to dismiss Ngouabi as paratroop commander. In retaliation, paratroops and militia mutinied and arrested the chief of the general staff, Major David Moutsaka, and other officers. In Massamba-Débat's absence from the country, Noumazalay set up new military structures under a National People's Army on the Chinese model. Massamba-Débat returned on 3 July to be greeted by government and party officials in battledress.

From the end of 1967 Massamba-Débat faced difficulties with both the army and the MNR. The military was reorganized into nine regions in order to divide its officer corps. In January 1968 Massamba-Débat decided to confront the party, sacking Noumazalay and abolishing the premiership. He accused young radicals of setting up an opposition movement and of 'intoxicating the army, the youth movement and the police in order to overthrow the government'. Massamba-Débat's challenge led rapidly to open confrontation. The president tried to rally support in rural regions but the MNR defied him in the towns. By late July he was offering to contest an election with anyone prepared to assume leadership. From July 31 to 3 August 1968, unrest flared up among army officers when Marien Ngouabi was arrested. When, on 1 August 1968, he ordered the dissolution of the MNR, he was forced to flee to his home village. Ngouabi took charge of Brazzaville as army commander and summoned the president to return.

On 5 August 1968, overriding the interests of the JMNR, Ngouabi and Massamba-Débat agreed on a temporary government under the control of a National Revolutionary Council (CNR), with Major Alfred Raoul as prime minister. By the end of the next week, the CNR under the chairmanship of Ngouabi abrogated the constitution and replaced it with a Fundamental Act. This paved the way for full military rule on 3 September 1968, when Massamba-Débat was effectively dismissed, tendering his resignation the next day. Alfred Raoul became acting head of state, but Ngouabi remained the real power behind the throne. In a government reshuffle that better depicted these realities, on January 1969 Ngouabi became head of state, replacing Raoul, who assumed vice presidency and premiership.

Ngouabi's aim was to transform his country into a socialist state. He developed close links with China and the Soviet Bloc. But the Congo continued to have shaky relations with its African neighbours, partially because of its revolutionary stance and partially because of the resentment felt by the other former French Equatorial African states over the Congo's pivotal position and more developed infrastructure on which they were dependent. A rupture of relations with Congo-Kinshasa (Zaïre) occurred in October 1968 as a result of one of the frequent quarrels between the two Congos. Diplomats would not be exchanged again by the two countries until December 1970.

The Ngouabi regime gradually ceded more power to the small

groups around the new president, although sustaining a radical momentum. A Marxist-Leninist vanguard party, the Parti Congolais du Travail (Congolese Labour Party or PCT), replaced the suspended MNR in December 1969. It was granted 'supreme power' but was now more tightly controlled by its political bureau and central committee, which was essentially the CNR. The country was renamed the Republique Populaire du Congo (People's Republic of the Congo) and its emblem, slogan and national anthem were changed. A new constitution was promulgated on 3 January 1970.

On 23 March 1970, an alleged invasion plot by Youlou supporter Pierre Kikanga, supported by thirty members of the gendarmerie, was swiftly defeated. As a result an extraordinary congress (30 March - 1 April 1970), the PCT dissolved the gendarmerie and resurrected the 'people's militia' as an adjunct to the army. The new militia was to be organized on Chinese lines as a security army of the party, politically and ideologically trained 'to ensure with fierce jealousy the fruits of the revolution'. The youth movement was also revived at the congress and renamed the Union de la Jeunesse Socialiste du Congo (UJSC). The aim of these changes was to bring the two organizations under effective party control.

Nonetheless, there were politically important student demonstrations against the government in 1971, culminating in a strike. It is important to note that the country's population is mostly young and has a long tradition of political activism. By the early 1970s it had been largely indoctrinated with Marxist ideas, and though inexperienced in administration the youth were politically influential. In many ways Ngouabi regarded their actions as a hidden political opposition. In response he promised extensive changes in party and government personnel, but also subdued the strikes with the army. Several ministries were abolished and ministers dismissed, including vice president Ange Diawara, premier Alfred Raoul, and foreign minister Auxence Ickonga. The political bureau of the PCT was cut from nine members to five and about fifty members of the party's central committee were expelled, including first secretary, Claude-Ernest Ndalla. These dismissals can be seen as a purge of the PCT's Maoist faction.

Ndalla and Diawara had been closely identified with the old JMNR and the associated Chinese-trained militia, and their removal was regarded as a setback for the extreme left. Both men were implicated in unsuccessful attempts to overthrow the Ngouabi government on 22 February and 17 May 1972. Diawara was sentenced to death *in absentia*. The chief of staff, Colonel (later Brigadier) Joachim Yhombi-Opango, was responsible for forestalling the coups. The relatively moderate Raoul was among the accused plotters, but the majority were militants who had participated in the overthrow of Massamba-Débat in 1968.

Although sentenced to nineteen years imprisonment, Raoul was released in August 1972 as a gesture of liberalism by President Ngouabi. However, the country was not entering the peaceful phase that the president anticipated, and by the end of the year there were signs that attempts might be made to disrupt the adoption of a new constitution and sabotage the new 'revolutionary' institutions that were to be set up under it. Trouble was developing in the south of the country, where there had recently been a wave of political murders, attempts had been made to steal arms from the army, and tribal antagonisms were being aroused by hostile forces. Unnoticed by many foreign observers caught in the leftist rhetoric of the Congolese elite was the brutal fact that the politics of tribal favouritism had continued unabated.

In January 1973 revolutionary courts tried a number of people accused of planning to endanger the security of the state. Shortly afterwards, on February 15, the discovery of a major plot was announced. Ange Diawara was accused of being behind it. More than 100 people were arrested and about half were retained in custody. A widespread purge followed. The police force was disbanded and its more reliable elements incorporated into the army, and a new people's militia was created. Any civil servants who appeared to be superfluous were dismissed, as were all 'unproductive' government employees. Revolutionary committees in industrial and other concerns were dissolved. Eight new judges were appointed to the country's highest court, including four members of the PCT's central committee. Those accused of involvement in the attempted *coup d'etat* of February 1973 were brought before this court in April. Sentences were passed on April 23 and included four of the death penalty. Writer Sylvain Bemba, who had been dismissed as minister of information because of his suspected involvement, was given a three-year suspended sentence. Pascal Lissouba, the former prime minister, was acquitted. Ange Diawara was again condemned in his absence. The next day it was announced that Diawara had been killed in a shootout with a Congolese army unit on the Congo-Zaïre border.

Ange Diawara's success in maintaining guerrilla resistance to the Ngouabi regime and evading capture for over a year despite the most most strenuous efforts of the Congolese army, led on one occasion by Ngouabi himself, indicated that the government was far from enjoying overwhelming popular support. It is significant that Diawara's base was among the peasants of the south; Ngouabi and most of his associates came from the north, and it would appear that there was resentment of their monopoly over the spoils of office. This ethnic tension, added to disagreements over political ideology and apparent power struggles within the political elite, helped to produce a continuing atmosphere of political uncertainty in the Congo. Plots and rumours of plots, redistributions of responsibility between the various branches of the governmental machinery and occasional violent outbreaks among the students and even schoolchildren of Brazzaville all testified to this instability. Relations with the West, which had deteriorated with the Congo's support for leftist revolutionary movements and its continued pattern of human rights violations, worsened with the regime's breaking of diplomatic relations with Israel on 31 December 1972. Little investment entered the country: that which did was from France and only served to enhance the former colony's dependence on its old imperial master. A bizarre combination of anti-colonial political rhetoric, pre-colonial ethnic division and neo-colonial economic reality had developed.

On 24 June 1973, a referendum was held to approve the new constitution, and votes were cast for the new People's National Assembly and for local government bodies. The constitution had been drafted at another extraordinary congress of the PCT in December 1972. It included provisions for the creation of a People's National Assembly, elected from a PCT list, and of local and regional councils, elected on the same basis, and for the appointment of a prime minister. Under its provisions power continued to be reserved to the PCT, but was divided slightly differently between the organs of government. The referendum showed popular approval of the constitution by 529,655 votes to 118,311 in an eighty-three per cent poll. The 115 members of the National Assembly received a slightly lower proportion of 'yes' votes in a larger ballot and were elected by 365,382 votes to 185,347. In local council elections held at the same time, the party's candidates failed to get an over-all majority in Dolisie (now Loubomo) and Jacob (now Nkayi), but they took up their positions nonetheless. The new bodies became operational at once. In August Henri Lopés, a former foreign minister and a member of the PCT's political bureau, became prime minister and formed a new government.

Understandably, one of President Ngouabi's major concerns was the control of the armed forces which brought him to power. The chief of staff Colonel Joachim Yhombi-Opango was dismissed in October 1973 and replaced by Captain Ondziel Bangui, who was himself dismissed in October 1974, making way for Major (later Colonel) Louis Sylvain Goma. At the same time Ngouabi took closer control of the armed forces, appointing himself head of a new supreme defence and security council. He carefully balanced socialist dogma with practical considerations. For example, in July 1973 he decreed worker participation in state and parastatal enterprises, but by 1 January 1974 new co-operation agreements with France were signed by a government which had become notorious for its radical pronouncements.

During the last five days of 1974 the PCT held its second ordinary congress, at which Ngouabi was unanimously re-elected chairman of its central committee and thus automatically returned as president of the republic. The following January, Prime Minister Lopés reshuffled his government and included a large majority of non-party members in the cabinet. The chief priority of the new government was to initiate successfully a three-year Development Plan for 1975-77, which had been endorsed at the PCT congress. It was also to oversee the purging of civil servants and agents of state enterprises which had been decided on at the party congress. Apparently President Ngouabi was dissatisfied with its performance as well as that of the party during 1975. In December he dismissed the PCT's politburo and the government. The politburo was replaced by a 'special revolutionary general staff' of five men, including the president and the new prime minister, Major Goma who formed a new government on 18 December. The ostensible reason for the reorganization was to curb corruption among state employees and to strengthen party and nationalized industry organization. As relations with the foreign oil companies worsened over declining petroleum production, in February 1976 the government demanded the renegotiation of exploitation agreements. There was widespread industrial discontent during early 1976, culminating in March with the arrest of trade union leaders on charges of fomenting a general strike.

Instability, Crisis and Change

After several attempts on his life, Ngouabi was assassinated on March 18, 1977, in what was claimed to be an unsuccessful attempted coup by supporters of the former president, Massamba-Débat. Another official version said that Ngouabi had been murdered by disloyal palace guards. There was a massive manhunt for Captain Barthelemy Kikadidi, the army officer alleged to be the leader of the assassination squad (he was captured and killed a year later), and there were numerous arrests, including those of Massamba-Débat and former prime minister, Pascal Lissouba. A military tribunal was set up to try the chief figures, and on March 25 Massamba-Débat was executed. On 23 March Cardinal Emile Biayenda, the archbishop of Brazzaville, had also been murdered in what appeared to be a revenge tribal killing for the assassination of Ngouabi since the attackers were identified as members of Ngouabi's Koulou clan. Ironically, Biayenda had been a strong supporter of national unity and had suffered house arrest under Massamba-Débat's regime. He may, however, have known the identity of Ngouabi's assassins, since he had apparently been in audience with the president shortly before his death. Much remains unclear as to what transpired in Brazzaville in mid-March 1977. It was not until February 1978 that Ngouabi's assassins were brought to trial. Ten death sentences were then passed.

Martial law was swiftly imposed by an eleven-member military committee of the PCT, and Colonel (soon to be Brigadier) Joachim Yhombi-Opango was nominated as the new head of state. On 5 April 1977, he announced a new council of ministers, abrogated the 1973 constitution, disbanded the national assembly (transferring their powers to the military committee) and announced that, as the successors of Ngouabi, the new leadership's policies would be a continuation of the old ones. The emergence of Yhombi-Opango, who was known for his opposition to left-wing critics of the regime, was greeted with some international enthusiasm. Low-level relations with the United States were resumed, a new agreement with France was negotiated, and cultural and economic pacts with Mozambique were concluded.

However, in 1977 an accident during exploration for carnalite deposits in the potash mines at Holle caused disastrous flooding, which forced the closure of the mining company and a dependent transport company. This represented a major blow to the Congolese economy. By 9 September 1977, the French and Congolese governments decided to liquidate the Compagnie des Potasses du Congo. Perhaps because of this economic dislocation, the government started to repatriate several thousand foreign workers and traders to neighbouring African states on 22 September 1977. In spite of protests from their governments at what the Mali foreign minister claimed was equivalent to the South African policy of apartheid, the repatriations continued steadily. In October 1977 all trading by foreigners was forbidden, and in early 1978 the heads of several state companies were arrested. Some state companies were closed down during this period, a process that continued after Yhombi-Opango's fall, and the ground was laid for a more liberal management of the economy.

Yhombi-Opango was accused of dictatorial behaviour and of encouraging corruption. His anti-left bias led him into open conflict with many important members of the PCT leadership. In August 1978 he announced the discovery of a plot against the government, and ten people were arrested including a former minister and a former National Assembly president.

Yhombi-Opango had difficulty in maintaining his authority and by early 1979 several important colleagues had turned against him. At a meeting of the central committee of the PCT in early February, Yhombi-Opango, after denouncing the divisions and intrigues in the party, handed over his powers and those of the military committee to the central committee of the party. A provisional committee, appointed to prepare the extraordinary party congress called to choose the new government, assumed power in the interim and asked Prime Minister Goma to handle day-to-day affairs. The president of the provisional committee was Colonel Denis Sassou-Nguesso, a follower of Ngouabi, longtime rival of Yhombi-Opango and leader of the militant faction of the PCT. When the congress was held at the end of March, he was appointed head of state, president and chairman of the central committee. A new council of ministers under Goma was announced on April 4. At first allowed to remain a member of the central committee, Yhombi-Opango was arrested and charged with high treason.

In July 1979 elections were held for a people's national assembly and for regional councils, while the proposed socialist constitution was overwhelmingly approved in a referendum. A month later, marking the 16th anniversary of the Congolese revolution, President Sassou-Nguesso decided to release a number of political prisoners, including those implicated in the assassination of Ngouabi in March 1977 and those accused in the plot of August 1978. The president also announced that Congolese living abroad who were opposed to the regime could return to their country without fear of repression. Later he rehabilitated some of those implicated in the Diawara plot.

The revolutionary rhetoric of the Sassou-Nguesso regime and its declarations of loyalty to Ngouabi-style socialism were belied by an increasingly pro-Western foreign policy and a correspondingly liberal economic policy. On 12 May 1979, soon after Sassou-Nguesso rose to power, full diplomatic relations with the United States were reestablished after a 12-year hiatus (1965-77). This shift was coloured by Sassou-Nguesso's ability to maintain a balance between the pro-Soviet upholders of Marxist orthodoxy and the pro-Western technocrats within the ruling elite. Cutting across this ideological divide was the tribal rivalry which continues to characterize the Congo's political and social life. The country's first two presidents were members of southern tribes but the three since 1968 have been northerners. Hence the development of the north is one of the priorities of the 1982-86 development plan. In addition to the north-south divide, there is factionalism between northern tribes, some of whom feel that they have not sufficiently benefited from northern domination. In this context, any change in the membership of the government or of the PCT's political bureau became a significant event by modifying the existing balance.

As the 3 October 1980 saw the celebration of the centenary of the founding of Brazzaville, the Congo began to drift away from its revolutionary stances. It is significant that Sassou-Nguesso's liberalization affected more than just those sectors of the economy which were opened to foreign investment. Peasant agriculture was emphasized, rather than state farms. Measures were taken from 1983 on to institute popular participation in justice. However, by April 1983 disaster struck Sassou-Nguesso's plans when the 1982-86 development plan was curtailed because of a fall in petroleum revenues.

At the third PCT Congress, in July 1984, Sassou-Nguesso was unanimously re-elected Chairman of the PCT Central Committee and President of the Republic for a second five-year term. Under the provisions of a constitutional amendment, he also became Head of Government. As a result of an extensive government reshuffle in August, Ange-Edouard Poungui, a former Vice President became Prime Minister in succession to Colonel Louis Sylvain Goma, who had held the post since December 1975. Sassou-Nguesso assumed control of the Ministry of Defence and Security. Legislative elections were held in September 1984. In December 1985, following a reorganization of the secretariat of the PCT Central Committee, the government was reshuffled again and its membership reduced. In November 1986 the membership of the Politburo was decreased from thirteen to ten, and in the following month the number of ministerial portfolios was again reduced by means of a government reshuffle.

Persistent ethnic rivalries, together with disillusionment with the government's response to the country's worsening economic situation, resulted in an increase in opposition to the Sassou-Nguesso regime during the late 1980s. In July 1987 some twenty army officers, most of whom were members of the Kouyou clan, were arrested for alleged complicity in a coup plot. Shortly afterwards fighting broke out in the northern Cuvette region between government forces and troops led by Pierre Anga, a supporter of ex-President Yhombi-Opango. In early September government troops suppressed the rebellion with French military assistance. Yhombi-Opango, who had been put under house arrest, was transferred back to prison. Anga evaded arrest. In July 1988 it was reported that he had been killed by the security forces. However, the vulnerability of the regime was demonstrated by the fact that once again an armed opponent roamed the country for a year after being identified.

Changes in the PCT hierarchy in July 1987 were followed by a government reshuffle in August. A further reallocation of cabinet posts took place in July 1988. In August 1988 an amnesty was announced for all political prisoners sentenced before July 1987, to commemorate the 25th anniversary of the overthrow of the Youlou regime. During August 1988 a faction of the PCT published a document accusing the Government of having lost its revolutionary momentum, and criticizing its recourse to the IMF and alleged links with the South African Government.

At the PCT Congress in July 1989, Sassou-Nguesso, the sole candidate, was re-elected chairman of the PCT and President of the Republic for a third five-year term. A new Politburo was elected, comprising thirteen members, six of whom were new to office. The Central Committee was reorganized to include 23 new members, who apparently held moderate views, while 21 of the existing members, considered to be conservative, were dismissed. Among those dismissed was Pierre Nze, a Marxist who had served under the regime of President Marien Ngouabi. In August Alphonse Mouissou Poaty-Souchalaty, formerly the Minister of Trade and Small and Medium-sized Enterprises, was appointed Prime Minister, and a new government was announced.

Legislative elections were held in September 1989. The single list of 133 candidates, presented by the PCT, was approved by 99.2 per cent of the voters. The list included, for the first time, candidates who were not members of the PCT; sixty-six were members of a front comprising youth, women's welfare, religious and professional organizations, and eight seats were reserved for unaffiliated individuals.

In November 1989 Sassou-Nguesso announced plans for economic reforms, breaking completely from socialist policies. Public-sector monopolies were to be transferred to the private sector, and private enterprise was to be promoted in order to attract both foreign and domestic investment. In December a new political movement opposed to the regime, the Union pour la Démocratie Congolaise (UDC), was founded by Sylvain Bemba. In the same month, forty prisoners who had been detained without trial since July 1987 were released. These reforms had been accompanied by a gradual but important shift in the country's foreign policy.

In spite of good relations between the two countries, the USSR did not provide aid to the Congo on anything like the scale it needed. Hence, since the mid-1970s the Congo has moved away from the Soviet sphere of influence, and has fostered links with neighbouring francophone countries, France, the USA and the People's Republic of China. France has continued to be by far the most important supplier of aid (more than one-half of total assistance to the Congo), as well as the major trading partner and business partner in the extraction of petroleum. Sassou-Nguesso accepted an invitation to make an official visit to Paris in October 1979, against the wishes of some of his entourage. His government reiterated its openness to Western aid and investment repeatedly. But the need, for domestic and party reasons, to maintain a balanced approach toward both the Western and Soviet blocs is demonstrated in Congolese diplomatic activity throughout the 1980s. A PCT delegation visited Kabul in February 1980 to meet Afghanistan's new Soviet-backed leaders. Relations with France further improved in 1981 when the Socialist Party came to power in France. President Mitterand of France visited Brazzaville on 10 and 11 October 1982. He was followed in January 1983 by the Chinese premier. In 1983 Nguesso visited both Zambia (10 July) and France (20-23 September). In October 1983, Georges Marchais, secretary-general of the French Communist Party, visited Brazzaville. From 23 to 25 November 1983, the King and Queen of Spain visited the Congo.

The Congo has continued to be an active member of the Union Douanière et Economique de l'Afrique Centrale (Customs and Economic Union of Central Africa or UDEAC). In December 1983 Sassou-Nguesso was elected president of the UDEAC for 1984 and visited Angola. March 1984 saw the signing of a trade agreement between Cameroon and the Congo and a visit by President Eanes of Portugal to Brazzaville. On 12 April 1984, President Samora Machel of Mozambique signed a treaty of co-operation at the end of an official visit to Brazzaville. Perhaps under French influence, the Congo established good relations with its right-wing francophone neighbours, Cameroon, Gabon and Zaïre. But it remains an important ally of Angola, whose government it assisted in the civil war of 1975-76.

The Congo is strongly committed to the Organization of African Unity (OAU) and participated in most of the committees that were set up to resolve the increasing divisions within the organization in 1982-83. Throughout the 1980s, it also contributed significantly to the diplomacy surrounding the war in Chad. In 1986-87 during his tenure of the OAU chairmanship, Sassou-Nguesso toured a number of Western European countries. In 1988 the Congo mediated in negotiations between Angola, Cuba, South African and the USA, which resulted in the signing, in December, of the Brazzaville accord, regarding the withdrawal of Cuban troops from Angola and progress towards Namibian independence. In April 1989 relations between the Congo and Zaïre became strained, following reciprocal expulsions from those countries of Congolese and Zaïrean nationals, who were alleged to be illegal residents. The immediate situation was resolved following a visit by Sassou-Nguesso to Zaïre. However, the expulsion of tens of thousands of Zaïreans in December 1991 and instability in Zaïre early in 1993 have led to a continuation of uncertainty in relations between the two countries. Ties with France were briefly strained in 1992 when Bernard Yanga, a key witness in the 1989 bombing of a French airliner, in which 170 people were killed, disappeared from his cell in a Congolese jail. He was believed to have been abducted by Libyan agents. However, relations between the Congo and her former colonial master have continued to strengthen.

The Congo has developed ties with Western countries other than France. An Italian company works one of the smaller petroleum deposits. The USA and the United Kingdom reopened their embassies in Brazzaville in 1983. In February 1990 President Sassou-Nguesso visited the USA; it was hoped that the Congolese government's plans for economic reform, announced in November 1989 would promote co-operation between the two countries. Diplomatic relations with South Korea (severed in 1964) were restored in June 1990. Even relations with the previously reviled enemies of Marxist revolutionaries, such as the IMF, Israel and South Africa, were not out of the question.

The 1980s closed with yet another crisis looming large. The continuing AIDS epidemic in equatorial Africa has taken a high toll in the Congo. Spread by the very transport system which has brought so many benefits to the country, HIV infection threatens to profoundly disrupt national life. In surveys in 1990, between six and eight per cent of adults in Pointe-Noire and four per cent in Brazzaville were infected. This is added to the already critical health problems of malaria, sleeping sickness, bilharzia and river blindness.

Political Transformation

The Congo's first constitutions, political parties, and labour unions were based on French models, but they were progressively 'Africanized' as ties with France were loosened. The Congo Republic's constitution of 2 March 1961 did not survive the downfall of its author, Fulbert Youlou: the constitution of 8 December 1963, sponsored by his successor, Massamba-Débat, was replaced by the Fundamental Act of 14 August 1968, after a military coup d'etat; and on 24 June 1973, the Congo's third president, Marien Ngouabi, won popular acceptance of his constitution setting up a People's Republic of the Congo. However, by the 1990s the entire Congolese political system was undergoing rapid transformation and further changes are likely in the near future.

Introduction

Until September 1990 there was only one authorized political party, the Parti Congolais du Travail (PCT). The Chairman of the Central Committee of the PCT was the President of the Republic, Head of State and Head of Government, elected for a five-year term by the Congress of the PCT, which also elects its Central Committee. To direct its policy, the Central Committee elects a Politburo, which comprised thirteen members when reorganized in July 1989. The senior executive body of the PCT is the Secretariat of the Central Committee, with four members. Supreme executive power rests with the Council of Ministers, under the chairmanship of the President of the Republic. The main legislative body is the National People's Assembly, which was re-established in 1979. Until 1991 its 133 members were elected by universal adult suffrage from a list proposed by the PCT. The Assembly was responsible to the Prime Minister, who was, in turn, responsible to the PCT.

Local administration was vested in nine People's Regional Councils, each with a centrally appointed commissioner and an executive committee elected by universal franchise. Regions are sub-divided into forty-six districts and six communes. Brazzaville forms a special capital district. Until 1990 these local units acted under the direction of ten commissars designated by the PCT Central Committee. Justice is administered by the Supreme Court, a court of appeal and a criminal court in Brazzaville and a network of lesser tribunals in the regions.

Progress towards political reform dominated the latter half of 1990. In early July the Government announced that an extraordinary Congress of the PCT would be convened during 1991 to formulate legislation enabling the introduction of a multi-party system. Measures were also approved that would limit the role of the ruling party. It was stated that, while the attainment of a socialist state remained the regime's ultimate objective, strict adherence to Marxist-Leninist dogma would be abandoned. The Congress also effected a restructuring of the PCT's Secretariat, whose membership was reduced, by half, to four. Among those who were not re-elected to that body was Jean-Michel Boukamba-Yangouma, who in February 1990 had stated that the introduction of a multi-party system would provoke disorder and ethnic rivalries.

In mid-August, on the occasion of the thirtieth anniversary of the country's independence, more political prisoners were released, including Yhombi-Opango and two military officers who had been arrested in the previous month in connection with an alleged plot to overthrow the Government. At the beginning of September a reorganization of some minor government posts was announced. In mid-September a congress of the Confederation of Congolese Trade

Unions (CSC) was annulled by the Government, following demands by that organization for independence from the ruling PCT, the immediate transition to a multi-party political system and increased salaries for workers in the public sector.

In response to a two-day general strike, called in protest by the CSC, President Sassou-Nguesso agreed to accelerate the process of political reform and to permit free elections to the leadership of the trade union organization. In late September 1990 the Central Committee of the PCT agreed to permit the immediate registration of new political parties. During late 1990 more than fifty new political parties were registered, including the Mouvement pour la Democratie et le Developpement, founded by Yhombi-Opango. In early December the Prime Minister, Alphonse Poaty-Souchalaty, resigned. On the following day, the extraordinary Congress of the PCT, which had been scheduled for 1991, commenced. The Central Committee of the PCT was expanded from 77 to 249 members, and Marxist-Leninism was abandoned as the party's official ideology. Also in December 1990 the National Assembly approved constitutional amendments fully legalizing a multi-party system with effect from January 1991. Shortly afterwards, President Sassou-Nguesso announced that a national conference to determine a date for multi-party elections would be held in February 1991. In early January 1991 General Louis Sylvain Goma was appointed Prime Minister (a position he had held between December 1975 and August 1984). The national conference went ahead as planned in February, when 1,500 delegates met to discuss the country's political future. Sassou-Nguesso was forced to name a new prime minister, dismiss the cabinet, rewrite the constitution and schedule free elections for 1992.

In 1992 the Congo completed a peaceful transition to multi-party democracy, ending decades of one-party Marxist rule. A specific agenda for this transition was laid out during the Congo's National Conference of 1991 and culminated in August 1992 with multi-party presidential elections. Throughout the year, a transitional government, headed by André Milongo, had succeeded in holding a constitutional referendum as well as local and legislative elections. Approved by eighty per cent, the Congo's new constitution includes a list of fundamental rights and liberties similar to those adopted a year before by the National Conference. Although often fraught with organizational and practical hurdles, the year's series of elections were generally described as free and fair by impartial election observers from many different countries and international organizations. During the transition in the first half of the year, former President Sassou-Nguesso remained in office in a ceremonial role and, as head of the former ruling PCT, was a major presidential contender. However, he did not win the presidential elections of August 1992 and the Congo's new President, Pascal Lissouba, was inaugurated on 31 August. In November, confrontations between the President and the National Assembly resulted in a motion of censure after which President Lissouba dissolved the Assembly. (The new constitution gives the President the right to dissolve Parliament in the face of persistent and serious disagreements.) Elections to form a new legislature are expected in 1993.

The Congo's armed forces played a pivotal role in the country's democratic transformation. The army supported the concept of a national conference and provided security for the delegates throughout its sessions. A concerted effort was made during the transition to reform and depoliticize Congolese military forces. Initially, the armed forces resisted the transitional government's efforts to restructure the military high command, and on three occasions military units occupied Congolese television and radio studios to impose broadcast censorship. This came to a head as a result of a mutiny in January. The Government acceded to the main demands of the military leadership, and once the lines between civilian and military authority were reestablished without bloodshed, the armed forces went on to play a generally constructive, neutral role during the elections. Many former military officers purged in previous years for refusing to support the PCT were reinstated. At the end of 1992, military leaders again played a constructive role by bringing opposing coalitions together in a neutral setting to negotiate a way out of a political impasse that might otherwise have led to violent confrontations and even civil war. Congolese military expenditures for 1989, the last year for which the US Army Control and Disarmament Agency conducted a detailed analysis, were estimated at between $76 and $90 million. While there is criticism that the army is top-heavy, anticipated reductions in the near future will occur more as a response to tight financial constraints rather than to a new policy designed to reduce the forces.

Despite short-lived tensions with the armed forces early in the year and confrontations between the government and the opposition late in the year, the human rights situation in the Congo saw significant improvements in 1992 under determined civilian leadership. The new Constitution provides citizens with a broad range of legal protections and extensive civil liberties, including freedom of speech, press, assembly, association, and political choice. It also establishes a number of new courts (not yet functioning) as a check on arbitrary executive power. While in 1992 many of these new freedoms were exercised fully, some persistent human rights problems continued, including credible reports of police and military brutality and harsh prison conditions. There was also continuing societal discrimination against women and against the indigenous pygmy villagers in remote parts of the country.

Conclusions

The Congo has suffered similar problems to many other newly independent black African countries. Like other former French colonies, its most obvious economic problems derive from a rapid population growth; galloping urbanization and unemployment; a sharp decline in food-crop production; and the coexistence of a traditional subsistence economy with a modern economy dominated by foreign capitalists and technicians. Like other newly independent African nations where oil has been discovered, the Congolese have overestimated its potential for developing their country and also have underestimated the ensuing drawbacks of excessive dependence on foreign capital, expertise, markets and food imports.

Among other major obstacles to the Congo's attainment of unity and nationhood are the persistent antagonisms among ethnic groups and regions. Together with conflicting external influences, these have prevented the population's integration, hindered the overall development of the country as a whole, and created chronic governmental instability. During its first decade as a sovereign state (1960-70), the Congo underwent two coups d'etat and about a dozen raids, abortive plots and frequent changes in leadership and political organization. It moved from a parliamentary system and free-enterprise economy to a single-party government professing 'scientific socialism', and then to a military regime with Marxist trimmings. Under misleading ideological labels, leaders of the Vili, Lari, and M'bochi tribes struggled for political power. At the same time, all of them tried to make their country independent, economically as well as politically, by playing the world power blocs against each other. In so doing, the Congo had the advantages of a strategic location, modern rail and water transport, an exceptionally literate population, and rare resources in timber and minerals. To some extent, however, these assets have proved to be liabilities. The country's easy accessibility has exposed it to conflicting forces, both political and economic, and its high proportion of educated youths, alienated from their rural surroundings, has proved to be an unproductive and potentially disruptive stratum of the country's society. The African continent has seen much of all of these difficulties.

However, the Congo has distinctive features that set it apart from its neighbours. The espousal of Marxist-Leninism by Congolese governments from the fall of Youlou until the early 1990s permitted

Introduction

Brazzaville to maintain what could be described as 'neo-colonial' relations with France without criticism from abroad. The contrast between the old official ideology as expressed in Marxist terms and the government's more pragmatic behaviour is shown in the welcome it has given Western capital and businessmen. Congolese leaders can be credited with drawing in large amounts of foreign aid from diverse sources and also keeping the Congo relatively free of entangling alliances. Despite its inefficiency and inexperience, the government is gaining more control over the economy. As the country is receiving a larger share of the revenue from exploitation of the Congo's natural resources, first potash and then petroleum, it should be able to widen its range of international manoeuvre and pursue the development of its economy in the interests of the entire population. AIDS, unemployment, the effects of three decades of authoritarian rule and the growing pains of fledgling democracy will undoubtedly cause serious difficulties for years to come. But more than anything else, the Congo's future as a politically united and economically viable nation depends on the elimination of tribal and regional inequities that have been the root causes of its weakness and instability.

Names and Orthography

The naming of ethnic groups, languages and nationalities is a matter of some confusion. Bantu languages commonly add the prefix 'ba' to the name of an ethnic group. Hence the domininant southern ethnic group in the Congo is the Bakongo. Languages are usually denoted by the prefix 'ki'. Hence the above group's language is Kikongo. However, exceptions to this rule are the Bakota (whose language is Ikota) and the Sangha, Fang and M'Boshi (these terms are used for both the people and their language). The term 'Congolese' is a political term used to describe people, institutions or things related to the nation-state of the Congo (a Congolese citizen, the Congolese government, Congolese wildlife, Congolese companies, etc.). Therefore, for example, one could say the Bakongo, who speak Kikongo, live in the Congo where they are Congolese citizens. This would distinguish this particular group of people from the Bakongo, who live in Zaïre and Angola. The above terminology has been used throughout this work.

The placenames associated with the Congo were generally standardized in the colonial era. Following independence in 1960 some were changed. The two most important of these changes were Dolisie (which became Loubomo), Jacob (which became Nkayi) and Fort Rousset (which became Owando.) Also important to the study of the Congo are the changes which have occurred in neighbouring Zaïre (formerly the Belgian Congo), where the name of the capital has been changed from Léopoldville to Kinshasa, Elizabethville became Lubumbashi and Stanleyville, Kisangani. These changes have been noted and where confusion may occur in works before independence I have added the current usage in parentheses following the colonial form. Also note that the Congolese have not followed the Zaïreans and Angolans in using the Portuguese name Zaïre to denote the Congo river. Hence I have used the terms Congo river, Congo basin, etc. throughout.

Names and Orthography

In French language works, the names for the various ethnic groups of the Congo often differ from those accepted in English, such as the M'Bochi (M'Boshi), the Oubangui (Ubangui) and the Sango (Sangha). French, Dutch and German personal names with prepositions have been alphabetized according to surname. Hence Van Wing and de Brazza and are placed under the 'w's and 'b's respectively.

The Country and Its People

1 **Congo: profile.**
   Anonymous. *The Courier*, no. 125 (1 Jan. 1991). p. 27-50
One of the best recent overviews of the Congo is provided in the January 1991 issue of
The Courier, formerly *The UNESCO Courier*, which contains nine articles on the
country covering politics, agricultural research, business, planning, tourism, forestry
and overseas co-operation.

2 **A survey of political, economic and sociological development in the Congo
   (Brazzaville).**
   US Joint Publications Research Service.   Washington, DC: JPRS, 1968.
   46p.
This translation of a number of articles from the December 1967 issue of *Europe
France Outre-Mer* provides an excellent overall summary of the Congo. Although
dated it contains a good deal of information which remains useful, as well as a
depiction of the country after independence and the period of the Youlou regime.

3 **Area handbook for the People's Republic of the Congo (Congo
   Brazzaville).**
   Gordon C. McDonald, (et al.).   Washington, DC: US Dept. of Army,
   1971. 256p. bibliog.
Part of the excellent area handbook series, researched and written by the Foreign Area
Studies Department of the American University, this one-volume reference on the
Congo includes information, statistics, illustrations, maps and graphs on a whole range
of topics: history, physical and human geography, ethnology, social structures,
religions, politics, governmental, administrative and military structures, education,
arts, economy, finance, trade, agriculture, industry and labour. Although published for
the US Army, this work has wide applications as a source of briefing materials, a
background text and a source of facts and figures on the country. Unfortunately,
volumes in this series are updated only after enough events (deemed significant from

an official American point of view) transpire to warrant a new edition. Hence, information on the Congo dates from the late 1960s (much of which retains a measure of accuracy) and current events and updated statistics are missing. A useful bibliography, tables, photographs and maps are included.

4 **Background notes on the Congo.**
US Department of State. Washington, DC: US Government Printing Office, 1988. 6p. maps.

A pamphlet which provides general facts and figures about the country, including material on geography, culture, history, government, political conditions, the economy, foreign relations, defence, US-Congolese relations and travel notes.

The Congo.
See item no. 521.

Encyclopedia of the Third World.
See item no. 523.

Travel Guides

5 **Afrique centrale les republiques d'expression Française.** (Central Africa: Francophone republics.)
Edited by Gilbert Houlet.   Paris: Hachette, 1962. 533p.

Though somewhat dated, this French-language guide to the Congo and the rest of French-speaking equatorial Africa provides good descriptions and evaluations of cities, sights, and other geographical and cultural features of interest to the traveller. Hachette has released updated editions of this work, but these have been abridged quite severely.

6 **Central Africa: a travel survival kit.**
Alex Newton.   Hawthorn, Victoria, Australia: Lonely Planet, 1989.
260p. maps.

This unique travel guide includes an account of the Congo on pages 138-157. It offers a historical, cultural and geographical survey of the country, and more importantly, it provides practical information on climate, visa regulations, currency, health, security, business hours, communications and transport to and from the country, and internally. More specific information on shopping, entertainment, sights, accommodation and dining is provided for Brazzaville, Pointe-Noire, the Loufoulakari Falls, Djambala, Kinkala, Matoumbou, Loubomo and Owando. Maps of the Congo and the major streets of Brazzaville and Pointe-Noire are included, as well as a few colour photographs.

7 **Congo post report.**
US Department of State.   Washington, DC: US Department of State,
1986. 11p.

Intended as a guide for American diplomats and their family members posted in the Congo, this report contains practical information about living conditions in the country in the 1980s. It is a useful source of tips for travellers and offers an insight into the diplomatic community in Brazzaville. The material included covers geography, climate, population, public institutions, history, arts, science, education, the economy,

3

Travel Guides

transport, communications, the media, health, the American embassy, Brazzaville, food, clothing, services, domestic help, religion, recreation, official functions, customs requirements, currency, taxes, and public holidays. There is also a short reading list and a map of Brazzaville. A number of interesting black-and-white photographs illustrate the text.

Background notes on the Congo.
See item no. 4.

Cities of the world.
See item no. 42.

Explorers' and Travellers' Accounts

Early and colonial (1500–1960)

8   Remarks on the country extending from Cape Palmas to the river Congo.
John Adams.   London: Frank Cass, 1966. 265p.

An early British explorer and trader on the west coast of Africa, John Adams made a total of ten voyages between 1786 and 1800. This reprint of his 1823 book, published in London, contains his records and observations of what is now the Congo Republic's coast.

9   Two trips to gorilla land and the cataracts of the Congo.
Richard F. Burton.   New York: Johnson Reprint, 1967. 355p. maps.

Originally published in London by Marston, Low & Searle in 1876, this book traces Burton's attempts to find a gorilla (after reading the accounts of Du Chaillu). Although his quest was unsuccessful, this work is anthropologically important because of the descriptions of the author's encounters with the Fang. Burton also describes his journey up the Congo River, probably no further than the vicinity of Brazzaville-Kinshasa. Two folding maps are included.

10   Les Belges dans l'Afrique centrale, voyages, aventures et decouvertes d'apres les documents et journaux des explorateurs. (The Belgians in central Africa: voyages, adventures and discoveries from the documents and journals of explorers.)
Adolphe Brudo.   Brussels: Maes, 1886. 3 vols.

This massive work provides an impressive background for studies of Belgian colonialism and contains much information on natural history and ethnology, as well as detailed accounts of the earliest Belgian-sponsored expeditions in the Congo region and elsewhere in Africa. Although the author concentrates on the region now comprising Zaïre (the former Belgian Congo), this work contains information on the Zaïre River basin equally applicable to the Congo and on competing French colonial efforts in the French colonies north of the river. Drawings, foldout maps and monochome and colour plates are included.

11 **Exploration and adventures in Equatorial Africa.**
Paul du Chaillu. New York: Harper, 1861. 531p.
Du Chaillu describes his travels throughout the Gabon-Congo region in search of gorillas, crocodiles, leopards, elephants, hippopotami and other fauna in a narrative that is valuable both as a travel account and as a natural history. Reprinted in New York by the Negro Universities Press in 1969.

12 **Wild life under the Equator.**
Paul du Chaillu. New York: Harper, 1869. 231p.
This version of du Chaillu's collected writings on his travels in equatorial Africa is intended principally for young readers.

13 **The country of the dwarfs.**
Paul du Chaillu. New York: Sampson, Low, Son & Marston, 1872. 314p.
The flamboyant du Chaillu explores southern Gabon, the Gabonese-Congolese border area and Loango in search of past acquaintances, primates and pygmies. This is the last book which Chaillu wrote on his African travels before departing to study and write on Scandinavia and Lapland. Reprinted in New York by the Negro Universities Press in 1969.

14 **A journey to Ashango-land and further penetration into equatorial Africa.**
Paul du Chaillu. New York: Harper, 1867. 501p.
Du Chaillu's further adventures in Gabon and the Congo are described in this book along with much ethnological and natural history material. Also included is an appendix in which Professor Owen of the British Museum analyses a collection of human skulls sent to the museum by du Chaillu.

15 **Stories of the gorilla country.**
Paul du Chaillu. New York: Harper, 1899. 292p.
A collection of du Chaillu's best stories of his journeys in Africa.

16 **Wild bush tribes of tropical Africa.**
G. Cyril Claridge. New York: Negro Universities Press, 1969. 314p.
Reprinted from a 1922 original, this traveller's narrative of the Bakongo is described as 'an account of adventure and travel amongst pagan people in tropical Africa, with a description of their manners of life, customs, heathenish rites and ceremonies, secret societies, sport and warfare collected from a sojourn of twelve years'.

17 **The Congo and coasts of Africa.**
Richard H. Davis. New York: Scribner, 1907. 220p.
Although concentrating on the area currently comprising Zaïre, the author of this descriptive travel account also includes material useful in the study of the early French

Congo. Illustrations are included which were drawn from photographs by the author and others.

18 Travels in the Congo.
André Gide. New York: Modern Age, 1962. 305p.

Voyage au Congo, suivi du retour du Tchad (Travels in the Congo, followed by a return to Chad), the French language original of this work was published by the Parisian publisher Gallimard in 1927. This edition of Gide's unique commentary on his travels throughout French Equatorial Africa in the 1920s was translated by Dorothy Bussy. Gide was a keen observer of French colonialism and African conditions.

19 Trader Horn.
Alfred Aloysius Horn. Garden City, New York: Garden City, 1927. 302p.

A. A. Horn, known best as Trader Horn, was an unsophisticated petty trader. An 'Englishman born in Scotland', he spent most of his life as a merchant in what is now the Congo, Gabon, Río Muni and Cameroon. Because of the extent of his claimed travels, his unpolished descriptions and his humble origins, many disbelieved his stories. However, much of what he described was later corroborated and virtually his entire account is probable when others' works are compared to his details of time, place, culture and the other events and personalities he mentions. Horn's memoirs were taken down and edited by Ethelreda Lewis when he was seventy-three years old. Interwoven with his highly detailed descriptions are fascinating elements of his personal philosophy, a unique world view which combines the attitudes of his British working class origins with the transforming experiences of a life in tropical Africa. This edition contains a foreword by John Galsworthy.

20 Travels in West Africa: Congo Français, Corisco and Cameroons.
Mary H. Kingsley. London: Macmillan, 1897. 741p.

Mary Kingsley was a remarkable English woman who travelled along the Atlantic coast of Africa as a palm oil trader in the early 1890s, visiting the Fang country of present day Gabon. Her descriptions of people, places, flora and fauna are vivid and witty. More than any other early traveller in Africa, she had an understanding curiosity about and love for the black African, and large portions of this work are devoted to the customs, attitudes, crafts and other aspects of the Fang culture. It is unclear whether she ever actually entered the area now comprising the Congo. However, much of her writings on the Fang and on the region's flora and fauna are equally applicable to the Congo. Material on de Brazza, Brazzaville and French colonialism is also included. Valuable appendicies document trade and labour problems, diseases, reptiles, fish, insects, shells, plants and the cloth loom, and there are numerous illustrations.

21 A report of the Kingdom of the Congo.
Duarte Lopez. London: Frank Cass, 1969. 174p. bibliog.

Duarte Lopez, a Portuguese traveller of the late 16th century, visited much of the Atlantic coast of Africa. Originally published in Rome in 1591 by F. Pigafetta, this is the earliest traveller's account of the Kongo kingdom. This edition is a reprint of the 1881 English translation by M. Hutchinson. The volume includes two folding maps, a note on cartography and nomenclature (p. 140-5) and a bibliography.

22 **À travers l'Afrique centrale: du Congo au Niger.** (To cross central
   Africa: from the Congo to the Niger.)
   Casmir Maistre. Paris: Hachette, 1895. 307p.

Written when Maistre was only twenty-six years old, this illustrated account of the
author's travels in 1892-93 describe France's plans to dominate both the Niger and
Congo valleys and thereby the western half of the African continent. As representative
of the semi-official Comité de l'Afrique Française Maistre was responsible for making
treaties which expanded French rule to the Oubangui-Chari (the modern Central
African Republic) and southern Chad. His account places the Moyen Congo and its
capital Brazzaville in its proper context as the important foundation to France's
colonial plans.

23 **Au Congo Belge, avec des notes et des documents recents relatifs au
   Congo Français.** (To the Belgian Congo, with notes and recent
   documents relating to the French Congo.)
   Pierre Mille. Paris: Colin, 1899. 308p. map.

This French language account of the Belgian and French Congos provides interesting
comparisons of the two colonies around the end of de Brazza's tenure as Commissioner
General of the French colony.

24 **Conférences et lettres de Pierre Savorgnan de Brazza sur ses trois
   explorations dans l'Ouest Africain.** (Lectures and letters of Pierre
   Savorgnan de Brazza on his three expeditions to the African west.)
   Edited by Napoleon Ney. Paris: Maurice Dreyfous, 1887. 363p.

This account, in de Brazza's own words, conveys his uniquely respectful attitude
towards Africans and his hopes for the peaceful development of the Congo. His
writings, speeches and acts as an explorer and administrator are in remarkable contrast
with what happened elsewhere on the continent and with events in the Congo after his
departure. Years later de Brazza would be called upon to investigate the abuses of
French administration and the outrages perpetrated by concessionary companies in
French Equatorial Africa. A few illustrations are included.

25 **Trente mois au continent mystérieux: Gabon-Congo et la côte occidentale
   de l'Afrique.** (Thirty months on the mysterious continent: Gabon-Congo
   and the west coast of Africa.)
   N. Payeur-Didelot. Paris: Berger-Levrault, 1889. 403p.

This account by a French traveller provides an account of French colonial attitudes and
of the situation in the Congo and Gabon at the outset of the colonization of the
interior of equatorial Africa.

26 **Through the dark continent.**
   Henry Morton Stanley. New York: Harper, 1878. 2 vols. maps.

Stanley's narrative of his journey from the Great Lakes region of east Africa to the
mouth of the Congo River is historically important, both because of the fame of its
author and as an overview of the region at the outset of Europe's scramble for the
African interior. The work is illustrated with ten maps and 150 woodcuts.

27 **Adventures and observations on the west coast of Africa and its islands.**
Charles W. Thomas. New York: Negro Universities Press, 1969. 479p.
Written by the chaplain to the United States Navy's 1855-57 African Squadron, chapter
twenty-four of this offbeat but important account deals with the coastal region of the
Congo and the mouth of the Zaïre River. Thomas describes the scenery, inhabitants,
geography, climate, harbours, the effects of slavery, the region's ethnology and
religious beliefs and practices. The author is opposed to the Catholic Church, and he
postulates that the area's 'relapse to heathenism' which followed the initial successes
of 16th century Portuguese missionaries was the result of the very nature of Roman
Catholicism. This edition is a reprint of the 1860 original.

Post-colonial (1960–)

28 **Equator: a journey.**
Thurston Clarke. New York: William Morrow, 1988. 463p.
In 1984 Clarke set out on a three year journey to visit each of the countries along the
equator. Beginning and ending with his travels in South America, his book vividly
recounts his adventures and the cities, cultures and environments which he
encountered along his amazing journey. Material on the Congo includes descriptions of
Brazzaville in Chapter 7 and transport between Brazzaville and Kinshasa in Chapter 8.

29 **The last Eden.**
Eugene Linden. *Time*, vol. 140, no. 2 (13 July 1992), p. 62-68. map.
The author of this well-illustrated account travelled to the most northern districts of
the Congo along the Ndoki river, where he and his group entered virgin forested area.
His experiences in this region where animals have never encountered humans are
related in the article, along with a discussion of the environmental issues at stake in
preserving the African rain forest in general, and protecting the Ndoki area in
particular. Colour photographs and a map are included.

30 **Sweet smell of mangoes, an artist looks at the French Congo.**
Sigfrid Sodergren. New York: Dutton, 1968. 157p. map.
Translated from the Swedish by John Hewish, Sodergren's description of his travels in
the Congo is strongly coloured by both his Swedish nationality and his artist's eye. The
original Swedish title is *Dans Mot Mork Botten*. Illustrations and a map are included.

Geography

31 **Atlas generale du Congo.** (A general atlas of the Congo.)
Académie Royale des Sciences d'Outre-mer.   Brussels: Académie
Royale des Sciences d'Outre-Mer, 1948-62. 31 vols. maps.

Although concentrating on the Belgian Congo and Belgium's Trust Territory of
Ruanda-Urundi, this valuable collection of maps includes important studies of the
Congo River also applicable to the Congo Republic. It was issued in portfolios with
accompanying French and Flemish texts. Most of the maps are on a scale of
1:5,000,000. The Académie Royale des Sciences d'Outre-Mer was known as the
Institut Royal Colonial Belge from 1948 to 1953 and as the Académie Royale des
Sciences Coloniales from 1954 to 1962.

32 **That crucial French connection.**
Anonymous.   *The Economist*, (31 Oct. 1992), p. 46.

As part of a year-long series on twin cities, this article compares and contrasts the
histories, politics and daily life of the capital of the Congo, Brazzaville with its Zaïrean
sister capital, Kinshasa.

33 **French Equatorial Africa and the Cameroons.**
H. E. G. Bartlett, (et al.).   London: Naval Intelligence Division, 1942.
524p. maps.

One of British Naval Intelligence's geographical handbooks, this work provides an
account of the geography, history, cultures and resources of French Equatorial Africa
and the French (East) Cameroons at the time of the outbreak of the Second World
War. Although dated as a geographical reference, this work contains information of
some continuing relevance, as well as of historical interest. Maps, including two
coloured folding maps, and other illustrations are provided.

34   **Atlas de Brazzaville.** (Atlas of Brazzaville.)
     Roland Devauges.   Paris: Éditions ORSTOM, 1984. [n. p.]. bibliog.
This collection of computer-generated maps accompanied by a bibliography is the only major recent atlas of the Congolese capital.

35   **Carte routiere du Congo.** (Road map of the Congo.)
     Institut Géographique.   Brazzaville: Institut Géographique, 1982. map.
This coloured map (scale 1:1,400,000) is the best recent map of the Congo.

36   **The river Congo.**
     H. H. Johnston.   London: Marston, Low, Searle & Rivington, 1884.
     470p. maps.
A general description of the geography, natural history and anthropology of the western Congo basin from the mouth of the river to Bolobo is provided by the author. Two etchings, three maps and over seventy other illustrations are included in this superb early work.

37   **La Republique Populaire du Congo: apprenons a connaitre notre pays.**
     (The People's Republic of the Congo: learning to know our country.)
     Office National des Libraries Populaires.   Paris: Éditions Classiques
     d'Expression Française, 1976. 63p. maps.
This short illustrated geography, which includes both monochrome and colour maps, also appears under the title *Géographie de la Republique Populaire du Congo* (Geography of the People's Republic of the Congo.)

38   **De l'Atlantique au fleuve Congo: une géographie du souspeuplement.**
     (From the Atlantic to the Congo: a geography of underpopulation.)
     Giles Sautter.   Paris: Mouton, 1966. 1,102p. 2 vols.
The Congo and Gabon feature in this study of the effects of under-population in the region between the Atlantic Ocean and the Congo River. This excellent French language text goes far beyond a simple account of geography and demographics to include much historical and cultural material.

39   **Géographie du Congo-Brazzaville.** (A geography of the Congo-
     Brazzaville.)
     Pierre Vennetier.   Paris: Gauthier Villars, 1966. 170p. bibliog.
Written by the leading expert on the geography of the Congo, this general geography text for the country is particularly good on the economic aspects of national life.

40   **Pointe-Noire et la façade maritime du Congo-Brazzaville.** (Pointe-Noire
     and the sea front of the Congo-Brazzaville.)
     Pierre Vennetier.   Paris: ORSTOM, 1968. 458p.
The geography and social conditions of the Congo's seaport Pointe-Noire and its environs are described in this French-language book by a noted French expert.

41 **Atlas de la Republique Populaire du Congo.** (An atlas of the People's
Republic of the Congo.)
Pierre Vennetier.   Paris: Éditions Jeune Afrique, 1977. 64p.
This excellent atlas of coloured maps is introduced by Guy Lassere.

42 **Cities of the world.**
Edited by M. W. Young, S. L. Stetler.   New York: Gales Research,
1987. 4 vols. maps.
This multi-volume reference is a compilation of current cultural, geographical, political
and historical information on cities in every country. Information on Africa is found in
volume one and details on Brazzaville are found on pages 162-177. The section
comprises a map of Brazzaville, a general introduction on the Congo, general
descriptive information on Brazzaville and more specific data on education and
recreation in and around the city. Information on Pointe-Noire, Loubomo and Nkayi
follows. The entire country is then profiled with sub-sections of information on
geography, climate, population, history, government, arts, science, education,
commerce, industry, transport, communications, health, clothing, services and local
holidays. The section concludes with a recommended reading list and notes for
travellers. This work is useful for both scholars and travellers, and contains numerous
practical details of relevance for foreigners intending to reside in the Congo.

Area handbook for the People's Republic of the Congo (Congo Brazzaville).
See item no. 3.

Bulletin de l'Institut de Recherches Scientifiques au Congo. (Bulletin of the
Institute for Scientific Research in the Congo.)
See item no. 515.

Cahiers d'outre-mer. (Overseas notes.)
See item no. 517.

Encyclopédie coloniale et maritime, volume V. (Colonial and maritime
encyclopedia, volume five.)
See item no. 519.

Encyclopédie mensuelle d'outre-mer. (The monthly overseas encyclopaedia.)
See item no. 520.

The Congo.
See item no. 521.

Encyclopedia of the Third World.
See item no. 523.

The Environment and Climate

43 **Atlas climatique de bassin Congolais.** (Climatic atlas of the Congo basin.)
    Franz Bultot.   Brussels: Institut National pour l'Etude Agronomique de
    Congo, 1971-72. 2 vols. bibliog.
Although focusing mainly on Zaïre, the entire Congo River watershed is covered in
this well-conceived atlas of coloured maps and other illustrations. The subjects
discussed in this work include precipitation, sunshine, humidity, dew, and air and soil
temperature.

The last Eden.
See item no. 29.

**Tropical forests, some African and Asian case studies of composition and
structure.**
See item no. 366.

Geology

44 **The geochronology of equatorial Africa.**
L. Cahen, N. J. Snelling. Amsterdam: North Holland, 1966. 200p. bibliog.

The formation of equatorial Africa's geological structures is surveyed in this general work.

45 **Quelques considérations sur le bassin hydrographique du Congo.** (Some considerations on the hydrographic basin of the Congo.)
L. Davreux. *Bulletin du Société Royale Belge de Géographie*, vol. 81, nos. 1-2 (Jan. 1957). p. 67-79.

This article is a good general introduction to the hydrography of the Congo river basin.

46 **Mineralogy and microgranulometry of suspending matter and of alluvial sands from the Congo and Ubangui rivers.**
P. Giresse, R. Ouetiningue, J. P. Barusseau. *Sciences Geologique*, vol. 43, no. 2-4. (1990). p. 151-90.

A recent study of sediments and suspended particles found in the Congo and Ubangui rivers.

47 **Oil and Gas Journal.**
Tulsa, Oklahoma: Petroleum Publishing Co. 1902- . weekly.

News of developments in Congolese petroleum production can be found in this periodical of the petroleum industry. Recent articles include material on the Amoco Group's Yombo field (5 August 1991, p. 22) and on an offshore desulfurization unit which permits gas lift operations (13 Jan. 1992, p. 35).

48   **The evolution of the Congo basin.**
   Arthur C. Veatch.   New York: Geological Society of America, 1935.
   183p. bibliog.
Veatch's early work on the geology and geomorphology of the Congo river region includes a wealth of diagrams, maps and other illustrations, and an eleven-page bibliography.

Flora and Fauna

49   Etude sur les fôrets d' Afrique Equatoriale Française et du Cameroun. (A study on the forests of French Equatorial Africa and Cameroon.)
A. Aubreville.   Nogent-sur-Marne, France: Section Technique Agricole Tropicale, 1948. 131p.

Aubreville was the leading botanical expert on French Equatorial Africa. This is a summary of studies related to the forests of the region, mainly those of the Congo, Gabon and Cameroon.

50   Flore du Gabon. (Flora of Gabon.)
A. Aubreville.   Paris: Musée National d'Histoire Naturelle, 1961-1973. 23 vols.

This exhaustive botanical work on Gabon is also useful for the plants of the neighbouring Congo.

51   Les bois du Gabon. (The forests of Gabon.)
A. Bertin.   Paris: Larose, 1929. 306p.

The similarity of Gabonese and Congolese tropical forests makes this work useful for those studying ecology, sylviculture and wood industries in the Congo.

52   A population survey of forest elephants (Loxodonta africana cyclotis) in northern Congo.
J. M. Fay, M. Agnagna.   *African Journal of Ecology*, vol. 29, no. 3. (Sept. 1991). p. 177.

This is the most recent of a number of studies conducted by J. Michael Fay and his research team. In this article the numbers of forest elephants in the northern Congo is estimated and their future evaluated.

53   **Gorillas in the Likoula swamp forests of north central Congo.**
     J. M. Fay, M. Agnagna, J. Moore.   *International Journal of
     Primatology*, vol. 10, no. 5 (Oct. 1989), p. 477-80.

Fay and his research team publish the results of their studies of the populations and
ecology of lowland gorillas in the northern Congo.

54   **Bois du Congo.** (Wood of the Congo.)
     J. Fouarge, G. Gerard, E. Sacre.   Brussels: Institut National pour
     l'Etude Agronomique du Congo Belge, 1953. 424p.

Complete with illustrations and tables, this reference work on the trees and wood of
the Congo basin is useful in the fields of botany, ecology, forestry and woodcrafting.
Intended for use by the Belgians in what is now Zaïre, it is also applicable to the
Congo.

55   **Les tsetses.** (The tsetses.)
     Emile Hegh.   Brussels: Imprimerie Industrielle et Financiere, 1929 &
     1946. 2 vols. maps. bibliog.

This study of the tse-tse fly, a pest common to the Congo Republic and much of humid
equatorial Africa, was compiled for the General Office of Agriculture and Livestock of
the Belgian Ministry of Colonies. The work includes illustrations, maps and
bibliographies.

56   **Birds of west central and western Africa.**
     C. W. Mackworth-Praed, C. H. B. Grant.   London: Longman, 1970 &
     1973. 2 vols. (African Handbooks of Birds series).

These well-illustrated identification guides for the birds of the western half of tropical
Africa include the Congo, and are the best English language reference works on the
ornithology of the Congo basin.

57   **Contribution à l'etude des poissons de la forêt de la cuvette Congolaise.**
     (A contribution to the study of the fishes of the Congo basin.)
     J. Lambert.   Tervuren, Belgium: Musée Royale de l'Afrique Centrale,
     1961. [n. p.].

One of the most comprehensive studies of the fish of the Congo river.

58   **Les poissons du Stanley Pool.** (The fish of Stanley Pool.)
     Max Poll.   Tervuren, Belgium: Musée Royale du Congo Belge, 1939.
     60p.

A brief illustrated guide to the fish of the Congo river around Brazzaville (Stanley
Pool) accompanied by a short bibliography.

59 **Les genres des poissons d'eau douce de l'Afrique.** (The types of
freshwater fish in Africa.)
Max Poll.   Brussels: Direction de l'Agriculture, des Fôrets et de
l'Elevage, 1957. 191p. bibliog.

This French-language guide to the freshwater fish of Africa, concentrates on former
Belgian-ruled territories, but those extensive sections dealing with the Zaïre River are
equally applicable to the Congo Republic. It is well illustrated and includes a
bibliography.

60 **Flore iconographique des champignons du Congo.** (A plant iconography
of Congolese mushrooms.)
Edited by Walter Robyns.   Brussels: Ministère de l'Agriculture, Jardin
Botanique de l'Etat, [n. d.]. 2 vols.

An eighteen-part study of the numerous species of mushrooms in the former Belgian
Congo (Zaïre) is presented in this reference work which includes fifty-five colour
plates. Most of the species described in this work are also found in the Congo.

61 **Contribution à l'ornithologie de la République du Congo.** (A contribution
to the ornithology of the Republic of the Congo.)
H. Schoutheden.   Tervuren, Belgium: Musée Royale de l'Afrique
Centrale, 1961-5. 8 vols.

Written in reference to the Belgian Congo (Zaïre), this is by far the best reference
work on the birds of the Congo as well.

62 **Note sur une collection de serpents du Congo avec description d'une
espece nouvelle.** (Notes on a collection of Congolese snakes with a
description of a new species.)
J. F. Trape, R. Roux-Esteve.   *Journal of African Zoology*, vol. 104,
no. 5 (Aug. 1990), p. 375-90.

This recent journal article describes some of the snakes found in the Congo, including
a new species not previously catalogued.

63 **Les phlebotomes du Congo.** (The phlebotomes of the Congo.)
J. Trouillet, G. Vattier-Bernard.   *Journal of African Zoology*, vol. 104,
no. 6 (Oct. 1990), p. 477-90.

A recent French-language study of Diptera and Psychodidae parasites in the Congo.

64 **Les plantes utiles au Gabon.** (The useful plants of Gabon.)
André Raponda Walker, Roger Sillans.   Paris: Paul Lechevalier, 1961.
614p.

Research botanists and economic development agencies would both find this guide
helpful, as it is geared both to the academic study of plant species and to their
economic potential. The similarities between Gabonese and Congolese flora make this
work useful for both.

65　**This mom teaches her young to walk on the wild side.**
　　Ken Wells. *The Wall Street Journal*, (22 March 1993), p. 1 & 6.
The newspaper article provides a good and surprisingly detailed commentary on a
orphanage project for lowland gorillas funded by a British charity, the Howletts and
Port Lympne Foundation, at the Brazzaville Zoo.

Two trips to gorilla land and the cataracts of the Congo.
See item no. 9.

Exploration and adventures in Equatorial Africa.
See item no. 11.

The country of the dwarfs.
See item no. 13.

A journey to Ashango-land and further penetration into equatorial Africa.
See item no. 14.

Travels in West Africa: Congo Français, Corisco and Cameroons.
See item no. 20.

The last Eden.
See item no. 29.

**Tropical forests, some African and Asian case studies of composition and
structure.**
See item no. 366.

Bulletin de l'Institut de Recherches Scientifiques au Congo. (Bulletin of the
Institute for Scientific Research in the Congo.)
See item no. 515.

Prehistory and
Archaeology

66 **Radiocarbon dates from west central Africa: a synthesis.**
    P. de Maret, F. van Noten, D. Cahan. *Journal of African History*, vol.
    18, no. 4. (1977), p. 481-505.

Little is known of the prehistoric past of the Congo, where efforts to find, classify and document archaeological evidence have often been inconclusive. In a worthy attempt to understand equatorial Africa's distant past, the authors of this article make an analysis of the data from archaeological dating tests gathered from 164 sites in the Congo, Burundi, Zaïre, Rwanda, the Central African Republic and Angola.

67 **The archaeology of central Africa.**
    Edited by Francis van Noten. Graz, Austria: Akademische Druck- und
    Verlagsanstalt, 1982. 225p. bibliog.

The 'first synthesis' of archaeological research works on the Congo, Zaïre, Angola, the Central African Republic, Rwanda, Burundi, Gabon, Río Muni and southern Cameroon, this work is supported with abundant photographs, maps, tables, charts and lists of radiocarbon datings.

History

Histories of Africa and west and equatorial Africa

68 **British views of the importance of French Africa to the Allied war effort 1940-1944.**
Barbara Baer. *Proceedings of the French Colonial Historical Society*, vol. 2 (1977), p. 16-23.
French Equatorial Africa was vitally important to the Allied war effort during the Second World War as a source of troops and raw materials, as a Free French base and as a bolster to the morale of occupied France. This article assesses the importance of this and other French African colonies at that time.

69 **Tricouleur: the French overseas empire.**
Raymond F. Betts.   London: Cremona, 1978. 174p.
This short book is a good introduction to French colonialism in English.

70 **Noir et blancs dans l'Afrique noire française: ou comment le colonisé devient colonisateur 1870-1914.** (Blacks and whites in French black Africa: or how the colonized became the colonizer, 1870-1914.)
Henri Brunschwig.   Paris: Flammarion, 1983. 243p.
This well-written and well-illustrated French-language book considers relations between Africans and Europeans during the first phases of French colonial occupation.

71 **The native problem in Africa.**
R. L. Buell.   New York: Macmillan, 1928. 1049p. 2 vols.
Described as a view of 'problems which have arisen out of the impact of primitive peoples with an industrial civilization', this somewhat racist examination of native

peoples, race relations and the effects of colonization looks at the post-First World War situations in French, British and Belgian African colonies and in independent Liberia. Much material is included on the Congo.

72 **The French presence in black Africa.**
Edward M. Corbett. Washington, DC: Black Orpheus, 1972. 209p. bibliog.

The history of French relations with, and influences on, both western and equatorial Africa is summarized in this good general work. A short bibliography is provided.

73 **African history.**
Philip Curtin, (et al.). Boston, Massachusetts: Little, Brown, 1978. 612p. bibliog.

This general history of Africa contains two chapters by Jan Vansina: 'Equatorial Africa before the 19th century' (p. 249-76) and 'A trade revolution in Equatorial Africa' (p. 419-43), which are of use to those studying the Congo.

74 **The Atlantic slave trade: a census.**
Philip Curtin. Madison, Wisconsin: University of Wisconsin Press, 1969. 338p. maps.

This work is one of many which seek to enumerate the human costs of the Transatlantic slave trade from the 1500s to the early 1800s. The lower Congo basin and Loango featured prominently in this grim commerce. Some useful maps are included.

75 **L'expansion coloniale de la France sous la Troisième République 1871-1914.** (The colonial expansion of France under the Third Republic 1871-1914.)
Jean Ganiage. Paris: Payot, 1968. 434p. maps. bibliog.

Ganiage's detailed description of French colonialism offers much information on de Brazza, Gentil and other personalities, events and the circumstances of French imperialism in the Congo and elsewhere.

76 **White man's grave: the story of the west African coast.**
L. G. Green. London: Stanley Paul, 1954. 249p.

Until improvements in medicine and sanitation in the 20th century, the Atlantic coast of western Africa was known by a variety of nicknames referring to the unhealthy state of the region, including 'death's waiting room' and 'the white man's grave'. Much stamina and courage was required of Europeans who ventured onto the west African coast. This general history is the story of European influence in west Africa and it provides an excellent background to the colonial history of the Congo. Some illustrations are provided.

77 **Histoire des colonies Françaises et de l'expansion Française dans le monde.** (A history of French colonies and French expansion in the world.)
G. Hanotaux, A. Martineau.   Paris: Société de l'Histoire Nationale & Plon, 1929-34. 6 vols. maps.

This history of French colonialism reflects the attitudes typical of imperialist sentiment in the years between the two world wars. Hanotaux had been French foreign minister during his country's era of aggressive expansion in Africa at the close of the 19th century. The maps, colour plates and other illustrations in this book are excellent.

78 **A history of the colonization of Africa by alien races.**
Harry H. Johnston.   London: Cambridge University Press, 1913. 505p.

H. H. Johnston, who was a British official in various parts of Africa, documented the colonization of the continent. Information on French colonialism in equatorial Africa and pre-First World War concessions to Germany appear in chapter nine, material on Christian missions is found in chapter ten and details on de Brazza and Du Chaillu appear throughout the book.

79 **French-speaking Africa since independence.**
Guy de Lusignan.   London: Pall Mall; New York: Praeger, 1969. 416p.

Translated from French, this is one of the best books in English on the first five years of Francophone Africa's independence. Much material on the Congo (including the Youlou regime, the Trois Glorieuses, and Massamba-Débat) is included.

80 **Francophone sub-Saharan Africa, 1880-1985.**
Patrick Manning.   Cambridge, England: Cambridge University Press, 1988. 215p. bibliog.

Manning defines Francophone Africa as 'a cultural community defined today by language' and stresses the general similarities of the seventeen nations included in his study without examining in any great depth the vast differences in religion, local language and geography of the huge region between Mauritania and Burundi. Six chapters are devoted to economics, politics and culture. Former Belgian colonies tend to be considered together with ex-French colonies, one of a number of points on which his thesis is open to challenge. However, he does provide a good background sketch of this important bloc of African nations, as well as many facts and figures. A good bibliographical essay is included.

81 **Black cargoes: a history of the Atlantic slave trade 1518-1865.**
D. Mannix, M. Cowley.   New York: Viking, 1965. 306p. bibliog.

This history of the Transatlantic slave trade looks at the Congo together with the more well-known areas of the west African coast.

82 **The first dance of freedom.**
Martin Meredith.   New York: Harper & Row, 1984. 412p. bibliog.

Meredith examines the difficulties and early failings of post-colonial black African nations. French colonial policy, the granting of independence to French Equatorial

Africa, the 1963 Congolese coup, the Congo's agricultural bureaucracy and the continued French role in Africa are all surveyed in this well-written book.

83 **France and the Africans, 1944-1960.**
Edward Mortimer. New York: Walker; London: Faber, 1969. 390p.

Mortimer's excellent political history of the last phase of French colonialism in black Africa includes much information and analysis of the Congo. Beginning with the Brazzaville Conference of 1944, this book examines the French Provisional Government, the First and Second Constituent Assemblies, the Bamako Congresses, French Africa under the Fourth Republic, elections, colonial reforms, the development of African political parties, constitutional issues, independent African governments and the French Community. The former French Equatorial Africa, which included the Congo, is frequently treated as a single unit in this work. However, specific information is also provided on the Congo during this era, including sections on the Congo's role during the Second World War and the Youlou government. In addition to its value in piecing together the country's history, this work is also valuable for demonstrating the position of the Congo in French-speaking Africa.

84 **The scramble for Africa.**
Thomas Pakenham. New York: Random House, 1991. 738p. maps. bibliog.

This excellent book traces the colonization of the African continent from 1876 to 1912. Although it tends to emphasize British imperialism and the activities of Belgian King Leopold II, a great deal of material is presented on French colonialism in the Congo. Chapter nine is devoted to de Brazza, Stanley and the French-Belgian competition to claim the Congo basin. Chapter twenty-nine deals with the extension of these colonies. Chapter thirty-two describes the abuses of the concessionary systems in both the Belgian and French Congos and the protest movements against these outrages. Chapter thirty-five discusses de Brazza's investigation into the administration of the French Congo, his death and the reform of the colonial system. This book is meant to show the European motives, activities and conditions which led to the division of Africa among the colonial powers. As such, it is a very readable, accurate, well-documented and uniquely comprehensive account. A chronology and valuable illustrations are included.

85 **Germans in the Cameroons 1884-1914**.
Harry Rudin. New York: Greenwood, 1968. 456p.

Described as 'a case study in modern imperialism', this reprint of the Yale University Press original of 1938 offers an excellent history of German influence and colonialism in the Cameroons until 1914, although it is regrettable that Rudin did not continue his study through to the aftermath of the First World War. Relations with the French and other colonial powers, border demarcations and German commercial interests are dealt with in some detail. Particularly valuable to those studying the Congo is the account of German efforts to acquire the Sangha river valley as a corridor to the Congo River. In 1912 these moves were successful and led to a recognition of German claims, which cut off Gabon and the remainder of the Congo from Chad and Oubangui-Chari (presently the Central African Republic). This division of French Equatorial Africa was quickly reversed by French and British actions shortly after the outbreak of the First World War.

86 **German imperialism in Africa**.
Edited by Helmuth Stoecker. London: Hurst, 1986. 446p.

This East German work (translated into English by Bernd Zöllner), covering German influences and imperialism in Africa from 1884 to 1945, adds details and a unique perspective to German colonialism. German attempts to create a vast central African empire are described as are German-French relations, German activities in Kamerun (Cameroon), the activities of German firms operating in Africa and pre-First World War concessions to Germany allowing Kamerun access to the Zaïre River via appendages through the present day Congo Republic.

87 **Afrique noire: occidentale et centrale.** (Black Africa: west and central.)
Jean Suret-Canale. Paris: Éditions Sociales, 1958, 1964, 1972. 3 vols.

A critical view of French colonialism in Africa is provided by this French-language work by a left-wing scholar. The three volumes of this work are divided into 'Volume One: geography, cultures and history'; 'Volume Two: the colonial era from 1900-1945'; and 'Volume Three: the post-Second World War era'. The work was revised several times in the 1960s and 1970s.

88 **French colonialism in tropical Africa 1900-1945.**
Jean Suret-Canale. New York: Pica, 1971. 521p.

This Marxist critique of French activity in Africa is Till Gottheimer's translation of the second volume of Suret-Canale's three-volume *Afrique noire: occidentale et centrale* (see item no. 87). Illustrations and maps are included.

89 **L'Afrique Équatoriale Française.** (French Equatorial Africa.)
Edouard Trezenem. Paris: Éditions Maritimes et d'Outre-Mer, 1955. 208p.

An illustrated French-language history of French Equatorial Africa and Cameroon between the mid-19th and mid-20th centuries.

90 **La fin de l'empire colonial Français.** (The end of the French colonial empire.)
René Viard. Paris: Maisonneuve Larose, 1963. 160p.

Viard traces the transition of French colonies from the Empire, to the French Union, to independence within the French Community.

91 **Black Africa and de Gaulle: from the French Empire to independence.**
Dorothy S. White. University Park, Pennsylvania: Pennsylvania State University Press, 1979. 314p.

Charles de Gaulle owed much of his success as war-time liberator of the French to the Congo and France's other equatorial African possessions. This book examines and analyses the General's relationship with black Africa before and during his presidency.

De l'Atlantique au fleuve Congo: une géographie du souspeuplement. (From the Atlantic to the Congo: a geography of underpopulation.)
See item no. 38.

Observations on the fevers of the west coast of Africa.
See item no. 213.

French colonialism 1871-1914: myths and realities.
See item no. 236.

Rulers of empire: the French Colonial Service in Africa.
See item no. 237.

La nouvelle politique indigène pour l'Afrique Equatoriale Française. (The new indigenous politics of French Equatorial Africa.)
See item no. 238.

Colonialism in Africa 1870-1960.
See item no. 239.

The rulers of German Africa 1884-1914.
See item no. 240.

France and Britain in Africa: imperial rivalry and colonial rule.
See item no. 241.

Transfers of power in Africa.
See item no. 242.

One hundred million Frenchmen: the assimilation theory in French colonial policy.
See item no. 243.

Les assemblées legislatives dans les etats de l'ancienne Afrique Equatoriale Française. (Legislative assemblies in the states of old French Equatorial Africa.)
See item no. 244.

The history of French colonial policy 1870-1925.
See item no. 245.

La politique Africaines du General de Gaulle 1958-1969. (The African politics of General de Gaulle 1958-1969.)
See item no. 246.

African boundaries: a legal and diplomatic encyclopedia.
See item no. 285.

A certain mystery: how can France do everything that it does in Africa – and get away with it?
See item no. 286.

China and Africa 1949-1970.
See item no. 288.

France in black Africa.
See item no. 289.

China's policy in Africa, 1958-1971.
See item no. 291.

La Mise en valeur de l'Afrique Equatoriale Française. (Investment in French Equatorial Africa.)
See item no. 294.

La crise economique au Congo Belge et en Afrique Equatorial Française. (The economic crisis in the Belgian Congo and French Equatorial Africa.)
See item no. 295.

False start in Africa.
See item no. 310.

Histories of the Congo

Pre-colonial (to 1800)

92 **Daily life in the Kingdom of the Kongo: from the sixteenth to the eighteenth century.**
Georges Balandier.   London: Allen & Unwin; New York: Pantheon, 1968. 288p.
Balandier's 1965 work, *La Vie Quotidienne au Royaume de Kongo du XVI a XVIII Siècles* (Paris: Hachette), was translated by Helen Weaver as this very readable book on the Bakongo and their history, which includes illustrations and a short bibliography.

93 **L'ancien royaume de Congo.** (The old kingdom of the Congo.)
Jean Cuvelier.   Bruges, Belgium: Desclée & de Brouwer, 1946. 361p. maps. bibliog.
Cuvelier's French-language history of the Kongo kingdom is centred on the early 16th century reign of Bakongo King Affonso Mvemba Nzinga, Portuguese influence and the missionary activities of the Roman Catholic Church at that time. This kingdom wielded power over parts of the southern Congo along both the river and coast. Maps and a five-page bibliography are provided.

94 **River of wealth, river of sorrow.**
Robert W. Harms.   New Haven, Connecticut: Yale University Press, 1981. 277p. bibliog.
During the era of the slave and ivory trade (1500-1891) the central Congo basin experienced profound changes. Harms examines the history of European commerce and investment in the region and the social, economic and political conditions which resulted. An eight-page bibliography accompanies this work.

95 **The Kingdom of the Kongo.**
Anne Hilton. Oxford: Clarendon Press, 1985. 319p.
An excellent historical and ethnological work with maps and references, this work is
essential to any study of the Bakongo and their history.

96 **The rise of Congolese state systems.**
Isaria Kimambo. In: *Aspects of Central African History*. Edited by
T. O. Ranger. Evanston, Illinois: Northwestern University Press;
London: Heinemann, 1968. p. 29-48.
Kimambo's chapter examines the pre-colonial rise of kingdoms in the lower Congo and
the adjacent coast.

97 **The history of Loango, Kakongo and other kingdoms in Africa.**
Liévain B. Proyart. In: *A General Collection of the Best and Most
Interesting Voyages and Travels in All Parts of the World*. Edited by John
Pinkerton. London: Longman, Hurst, Rees & Orme, 1808-14. vol. 16.
390p.
One of the most powerful states on the Atlantic coast of equatorial Africa during the
era of the slave trade was the Vili-dominated Kingdom of Loango, which, along with
the neighbouring state of Kakongo, covered much of the southern and coastal areas of
the present-day Congo. This account of the region is a translation of Proyart's 1776
work, originally published in Paris by Berton and Craport. It was included by
Pinkerton in an impressive seventeen volume collection of early explorers' accounts, of
which volumes 15 and 16 were also published as a separate work in 1819.

98 **L'ancien royaume du Congo des origines à la fin du XIXe siècle.** (The old
kingdom of the Congo from its origins to the end of the nineteenth
century.)
W. G. L. Randles. Paris, The Hague: Mouton, 1968. 276p. bibliog.
Concentrating on the Bakongo area of modern Zaïre up to 1908, this book offers some
insights into the history and cultures of the Congo, as well as illustrations, maps and a
bibliography (p. 237-64).

99 **The dark kingdoms: the impact of white civilization on three great
African monarchies.**
Alan Scholefield. New York: Morrow, 1975. 194p.
This illustrated work is a comparative historical study of the effects of European
influence on three traditional African monarchies: the Kongo, Benin and Lesotho.
Interesting, unique in its approach and valuable to scholars of African history, this
book introduces these three states for deeper study.

100 **The Kingdom of Kongo.**
John K. Thornton. Madison, Wisconsin: University of Wisconsin
Press, 1983. 191p. maps. bibliog.
Although the heartland of the Kingdom of Kongo lay mainly in present day Zaïre and
Angola, its boundaries crossed the Zaïre River and included parts of present day

Congo. Furthermore, this important African state of early modern times influenced, and at times ruled, the entire Congolese coastal area. This work, a revision of the author's PhD thesis, concentrates on the period of civil war and transition between 1641 and 1718. Chapters include information on the natural environment, society, political organization, economy and philosophy of the kingdom; the causes and history of the civil war; and the period of restoration which followed. Several maps, a glossary of Kikongo terms and a ten-page bibliography are provided.

A report of the Kingdom of the Congo.
See item no. 21.

Paths in the rainforests.
See item no. 235.

Colonial (1800-1960)

101 **Etude historique: la formation de la colonie du Congo Français: 1843-1882.** (Historical study: the formation of the French Congo colony: 1843-1882.)
Jacques Ancel. *Renseignements Coloniaux et Documents, Afrique Française*, nos. 4, 5 & 6 (1902), p. 79-94; 99-120 & 132-4 respectively.
This series of articles documents the establishment of French claims to the Congo and Gabon.

102 **De Brazza à Gentil: la politique Française en Haute-Sangha à la fin du XIXe siècle.** (De Brazza to Gentil: French politics in Upper Sangha to the end of the 19th century.)
Catherine Coquery-Vidrovitch. *Revue Française d'Histoire d'Outre-Mer*, vol. 52 (1965), p. 22-40.
Looking at the northern Congo, Coquery-Vidrovitch describes the arrival and impact of the French on this remote region.

103 **The river Congo.**
Peter Forbath. New York: Houghton Mifflin, 1977. 404p. bibliog.
Described as the story of 'the discovery, exploration and exploitation of the world's most dramatic river', this popular book is frequently found in libraries. It is a good introduction to the colonial history of the region, but the history of the Congo (Brazzaville) is sketched out in far less detail than that of Zaïre.

104 **George Grenfell and the Congo.**
Harry H. Johnston. New York: D. Appleton, 1910. 2 vols.
Grenfell, a British missionary was stationed for sixteen years in the Belgian Congo at Bolobo, a town in the northern part of Stanley Pool district across the river from the French territories. Although primarily concerned with the Belgian rather than the French Congo, this lengthy book provides a great deal of information on the French colony, which both Grenfell and his biographer Johnston visited several times. The

work includes much material on explorers, missionaries, ethnic groups, wildlife and other historical, cultural and natural aspects of the Congo basin. Both Grenfell's and Johnston's ideas are thought-provoking and the descriptions of the area are vivid. However, the reader is sometimes confused as to whose words are which.

105 **Brazza et la fondation de l'Afrique Equatoriale Française.** (Brazza and the founding of French Equatorial Africa.)
René Maran. Paris: Gallimard, 1941. 304p.

Centred on the life of de Brazza, this book surveys the European discovery, exploration and colonialization of French Equatorial Africa. Illustrations and a folding map are included.

106 **History of the Congo Reform Movement.**
Edmund D. Morel. Oxford: Clarendon Press, 1968. 289p. map.
bibliog.

Although this work concentrates on Belgian King Leopold II's Congo Free State administration, material is included on British writer Morel's investigations into the concessionary system in the French Congo. His publication of the abuses of these systems led to calls for reform and to increased American and European public opposition to colonialism. This presentation of Morel's work was edited by William Roger Louis and Jean Stengers and includes Louis' 'Morel and the Congo Reform Association' and Stengers' 'Morel and Belgium'.

107 **The British case in the French Congo.**
Edmund D. Morel. New York: Negro Universities Press, 1969. 215p.
map.

This is a reprint of Morel's 1903 original (London: Heinemann), in which he investigated the abusive concessionary system established in the French Congo under the administration of Commissioner General Gentil.

108 **L'expansion coloniale au Congo Français.** (Colonial expansion in the French Congo.)
Fernand Rouget. Paris: Larose, 1906. 942p.

This lengthy and sometimes difficult book is an early attempt to document French imperialism in equatorial Africa. However, it offers an accurate impression of French plans, expectations and attitudes of the time.

109 **L'affair du Congo, 1905.** (The Congo affair, 1905.)
Jules Saintoyant. Paris: Éditions de l'Epic, 1960. 162p.

The scandals of colonial abuse which rocked both the Belgian and French Congos are described in this work by a French author.

110 **The Tio Kingdom of the middle Congo: 1880-1892.**
Jan Vansina. London: Oxford University Press, 1973. 586p. maps.
bibliog.

Vansina's history of the Bateke kingdom of the central Congo and adjacent Zaïre includes much ethnological material, as well as maps, illustrations and a ten page bibliography. This work provides an excellent account of a people often overlooked by scholars, who have tended to concentrate their studies on the region further downstream, on the Bakongo who have been more accessible to Europeans.

111 **Congo.**
Richard West. New York: Holt Rinehart & Winston, 1972. 304p. bibliog.
This highly readable history of the Congo is centred on the life and accomplishments of Count Pierre Savorgnan de Brazza, within the framework of a concise history of the Congo up to independence. The author also includes extensive biographical information on other figures such as du Chaillu, Stanley, Morel and others.

The Congo and coasts of Africa.
See item no. 17.

Travels in the Congo.
See item no. 18.

Trader Horn.
See item no. 19.

Travels in West Africa: Congo Français, Corisco and Cameroons.
See item no. 20.

À travers l'Afrique centrale: du Congo au Niger. (To cross central Africa: from the Congo to the Niger.)
See item no. 22.

Au Congo Belge, avec des notes et des documents recents relatifs au Congo Français. (To the Belgian Congo, with notes and recent documents relating to the French Congo.)
See item no. 23.

Conférences et lettres de Pierre Savorgnan de Brazza sur ses trois explorations dans l'Ouest Africain. (Lectures and letters of Pierre Savorgnan de Brazza on his three expeditions to the African west.)
See item no. 24.

Trente mois au continent mystérieux: Gabon-Congo et la côte occidentale de l'Afrique. (Thirty months on the mysterious continent: Gabon-Congo and the west coast of Africa.)
See item no. 25.

Through the dark continent.
See item no. 26.

Adventures and observations on the west coast of Africa and its islands.
See item no. 27.

Histoire économique du Congo 1880-1968. (An economic history of the Congo 1880-1968.)
See item no. 293.

The concession policy in the French Congo and the British reaction 1897-1906.
See item no. 296.

Le Còngo au temps des grandes compagnies concessionnaires 1898-1930. (The Congo in the time of the great concessionary companies 1898-1930.)
See item no. 297.

The external trade of the Loango coast 1576-1870.
See item no. 298.

La Compagnie de l'Ogooué: son influence géographique au Gabon et au Congo. (The Ogooue company: its geographical influence on Gabon and the Congo.)
See item no. 299.

The black man's burden: African colonial labor on the Congo and Ubangi rivers 1880-1900.
See item no. 370.

Education in French Equatorial Africa, 1842-1945.
See item no. 378.

Brazza explorateur: l'Ogooué 1875-1879. (Brazza explorer: the Ogooué 1875-1879.)
See item no. 498.

Brazza explorateur: les traités Makoko 1880-1882. (Brazza explorer: the Makoko treaties 1880-1882.)
See item no. 499.

Congo explorer, Pierre Savorgnan de Brazza: 1852-1905.
See item no. 500.

Félix Eboué: gouverneur et philosophe. (Felix Eboué: governor and philosopher.)
See item no. 501.

Brazza et la prise de possession du Congo. (Brazza and the acquisition of the Congo.)
See item no. 502.

Les constructeurs de la France d'outre-mer. (The builders of France overseas.)
See item no. 503.

Au Congo Français: Monseigneur Carrie, 1842-1904. (To the French Congo: Monsignor Carrie, 1842-1904.)
See item no. 504.

John Holt: a British merchant in West Africa in the era of imperialism.
See item no. 506.

Félix Tchicaya: premier parlementaire Congolais (1903-1961), in memoriam. (Felix Tchicaya: first Congolese parliamentarian [1903-1961], in memoriam.) *See* item no. 508.

André Matsoua: fondateur du mouvement de liberation du Congo. (André Matswa: founder of the Congo's liberation movement.) *See* item no. 509.

Paul du Chaillu: gorilla hunter. *See* item no. 511.

Eboué. *See* item no. 512.

Brazza of the Congo. *See* item no. 513.

Cahiers d'études Africaines. (African studies notes.) *See* item no. 516.

Chroniques d'Outre-Mer. (Overseas chronicles.) *See* item no. 518.

Encyclopédie coloniale et maritime, volume V. (Colonial and maritime encyclopedia, volume five.) *See* item no. 519.

Encyclopédie mensuelle d'outre-mer. (The monthly overseas encyclopaedia.) *See* item no. 520.

A historical dictionary of the People's Republic of the Congo. *See* item no. 526.

Bibliographie de l'Afrique Equatoriale Française. (A bibliography of French Equatorial Africa.) *See* item no. 528.

Materials on west African history in French archives. *See* item no. 529.

Guide bibliographique sommaire d'histoire militaire et coloniale Françaises. (A concise bibliographic guide to French military and colonial history.) *See* item no. 530.

Bibliographie d'histoire coloniale, 1900-1930, Belgique. (A bibliography of colonial history, 1900-1930 – Belgium.) *See* item no. 532.

Official publications of French Equatorial Africa, French Cameroons and Togo, 1946-1958. *See* item no. 534.

Post-colonial (1960-)

112 **Black Africa at the turning point of its destiny.**
Jacques Arnault. *US Joint Publications Research Service Translations on Africa*, no. 81 (1964), p. 5-20.

Focussing on the Congo and its hopes for the future, this is a translation of three articles by Arnault which appeared in *L'Humanité* (Paris), no. 25, 27 & 29 (June 1964).

113 **The Republic of the Congo (Brazzaville): the hour of independence.**
French Embassy to the United States. New York: Service de Presse et d'Information, 1961. 32p.

This short, illustrated booklet was published by the French government to mark the occasion of Congolese independence.

114 **Abortive coup and economic program discussed.**
Mehdi Kader. *US Joint Publications Research Service Translations on Africa*, no. 857 (1971), p. 49-63.

The early plans of and threats to the Ngouabi regime are discussed in this translation of a series of articles which appeared in *El Moudjahid* (Algiers) throughout December 1969.

115 **Histoire du Congo.** (A history of the Congo.)
Marcel Soret. Paris: Berger-Levrault, 1978. 237p. maps. bibliog.

This French-language work is one of the best histories of the Congo. Soret is particularly strong on 20th century Congolese history. His distinguished background in demography and urban problems is also apparent in this account.

116 **Histoire et sociologie politiques du Congo.** (A history and political sociology of the Congo.)
Jean-Michel Wagret. Paris: Librairie Générale de Droit et de Jurisprudence, 1963. 250p. bibliog.

The politics and society of the newly independent Congo are described in this well-illustrated book.

Area handbook for the People's Republic of the Congo (Congo Brazzaville).
See item no. 3.

Benin, the Congo, Burkina Faso: economics, politics and society.
See item no. 247.

The development of political parties in French Equatorial Africa.
See item no. 248.

Four equatorial states.
See item no. 249.

Le Congo, formation sociale et mode developpement economique. (The Congo, social formation and economic development.)
See item no. 251.

Ideological rhetoric and scientific socialism in Benin and Congo-Brazzaville.
See item no. 252.

The politics of Congo-Brazzaville.
See item no. 253.

Political integration in French-speaking Africa.
See item no. 254.

Clan loyalties and socialist doctrine in the People's Republic of the Congo.
See item no. 257.

The Congo (Brazzaville) and neo-colonialism.
See item no. 269.

The emerging states of French Equatorial Africa.
See item no. 270.

Patrimonialism and changes in the Congo.
See item no. 271.

J'accuse la Chine. (I accuse China.)
See item no. 272.

Comment sauver l'Afrique. (How to save Africa.)
See item no. 273.

Histoire économique du Congo 1880-1968. (An economic history of the Congo 1880-1968.)
See item no. 293.

Personnalités publiques de l'Afrique centrale: Cameroun, RCA, Congo, Gabon, Tchad. (Public personalities in central Africa, Cameroon, Central African Republic, Congo, Gabon, Chad.)
See item no. 497.

A cardinal who spoke truth to power.
See item no. 505.

La vie de Marien Ngouabi: 1938-1977. (The life of Marien Ngouabi: 1938-1977.)
See item no. 507.

Félix Tchicaya: premier parlementaire Congolais (1903-1961), in memoriam. (Felix Tchicaya: first Congolese parliamentarian [1903-1961], in memoriam.)
See item no. 508.

The new Africans.
See item no. 510.

Africa research bulletin.
See item no. 514.

Cahiers d'études Africaines. (African studies notes.)
See item no. 516.

Keesing's contemporary archives.
See item no. 522.

Africa contemporary record.
See item no. 524.

A historical dictionary of the People's Republic of the Congo.
See item no. 526.

Population

117 **Etude démographique de quelques villages Likouala.** (A demographic
   study of some Likouala villages.)
   Jean M. Crocquevieille. *Population*, (Paris), vol. 8, no. 3 (July-Sept.
   1953), p. 491-510.
This article documents a population study in a remote area of the northern Congo.

118 **World population growth and aging.**
   Nathan Keyfitz, Wilhelm Flieger. Chicago: University of Chicago
   Press, 1990. 608p.
This excellent reference on world population trends contains in-depth material on the
Congo, including tables and graphs tabulating population figures since 1950, and
projections to 2020. The information covers mortality, fertility and ageing measures;
and urbanization, sex and life expectancy data.

119 **International population census publications, Congo (Brazzaville).**
   Population Research Center (University of Texas at Austin). New
   Haven, Connecticut: Research Publications, 1973-4. 3 series of
   microfilm reels.
A historical record of Congolese population statistics can be found in these collections
of 35mm microfilms, in which the censuses for 1945-67 are found in Series I, pre-1945
censuses in Series II and post-1967 censuses in Series III.

120 **Démographie et problèmes urbains en AEF: Poto-Poto, Bacongo,
   Dolisie.** (Demography and urban problems in French Equatorial Africa:
   Poto-Poto, Bakongo, Dolisie.)
   Marcel Soret. Montpellier, France: Imprimerie Charité, 1954. 134p.
The population dynamics of three localities in the southern Congo are described in this
illustrated book.

121 **Demographic, ethnological and other sociological data on the Congo (Brazzaville.)**
Jean-Michel Wagret. *US Joint Publications Research Service Translations on Africa*, no. 265 (1965), 82p. maps.

A good survey of Congolese society, this work is translation of a monograph issued by the Libraire Générale de Droit et de Jurisprudence (Paris: 1965).

De l'Atlantique au fleuve Congo: une géographie du souspeuplement. (From the Atlantic to the Congo: a geography of underpopulation.)
See item no. 38.

Cahiers d'outre-mer. (Overseas notes.)
See item no. 517.

Encyclopedia of the Third World.
See item no. 523.

Ethnic Groups

122 **Le groupe dit 'Pahouin'.** (The group called 'Pahouin'.)
Pierre Alexandre, Jacques Binet.   Paris: Presses Universitaires de
France, 1958. 152p. maps. bibliog.

The use of the term 'Pahouin' to mean Fang is unclear in origin but this mysterious and
enigmatic group, which inhabits the area from the Congo Republic, through Gabon
and Río Muni and into Cameroon, has fascinated many European scholars. In this
classic French work on the Fang and related groups, Alexandre and Binet present a
wide-ranging account of the tribe, its language, background, folklore and beliefs. Maps
and tables are included.

123 **Les Bongo-Rimba.** (The Bongo-Rimba.)
Efraim Andersson.   Uppsala, Sweden: Almqvist & Wiksell, 1983.
128p.

This French-language ethnology of the Bongo-Rimba and other pygmies in the Gabon-
Congo-Zaïre region includes a two-page bibliography and an English language abstract
(p. 128).

124 **Ethnologie religieuse des Kuta, mythologie et folklore.** (A religious
ethnology of the Bakota: mythology and folklore.)
Efraim Andersson.   Uppsala, Sweden: Almqvist & Wiksell, 1987.
164p.

The religious beliefs, folklore and oral literature of the Bakota of Gabon and the
Congo are the subject of this French-language study published in Sweden. The Bakota
are a group of tribes sharing a common tongue, but believed to be of mixed origins.
Their religious beliefs and material culture are strongly influenced by their forest
environment and by the neighbouring Fang tribe whose entry into Gabon over the last
few centuries pushed the Bakota south, mainly within Gabon, but also into the Congo.

125 **A dictionary of black African civilization.**
Edited by Georges Balandier, Jacques Maquet.   New York: Leon
Amiel, 1974. 350p.
This general reference work offers good but brief descriptions of the Fang, Bateke, Bakongo and other ethnic groups found in the Congo. The compilers are leading French Africanists.

126 **La civilisation des peuples Batéké.** (The civilization of the Bateke
peoples.)
Claude Cabrol, Raoul Lehuard.   Libreville: Multipress; Paris:
Éditions Paul Bory, 1976. 96p.
The Bateke are a seldom-studied Congolese ethnic group. This short French-language work is an excellent introduction to the tribe.

127 **The migration of the Fang into central Gabon during the nineteenth
century: a new interpretation.**
Christopher Chamberlain.   *International Journal of African Historical
Studies*, vol. xi, no. 3 (1978), p. 429-456.
Much scholarly speculation has been focused on the origins of the Fang tribe. Early writers mistakenly thought that they were nomadic. Others claimed that the group was displaced from lands to the north by the Fulani jihads of the 1700s. They were believed to have arrived in the forests of equatorial Africa (Cameroon, Gabon, Río Muni and the Congo) around the same time as Europeans were exploring the adjacent coast (1820 to 1890). Chamberlain analyses these theories and presents a probable history which combines a number of these strands of thinking.

128 **Savage man in central Africa: a study of primitive races in the French
Congo.**
Adolphe Louis Cureau.   London: Unwin, 1915. 351p. map.
Translated from the French by E. Andrews, this early ethnology of the peoples of French Equatorial Africa is intriguing, in spite of its many common prejudices of the colonial era.

129 **Africa and the West: intellectual responses to European culture.**
Edited by Philip D. Curtin.   Madison, Wisconsin: University of
Wisconsin Press, 1972. 259p. bibliog.
This excellent general work on European influences and African reactions to them includes a chapter on 'Fang representations under acculturation' by James Fernandez (p. 3-48).

130 **At the back of the black man's mind.**
Richard E. Dennett.   London: Frank Cass, 1968. 288p.
Sub-titled 'Notes on the Kingly Office in West Africa' and originally published in 1906, Dennett's book is an ethnology of the peoples of the Congo, Gabon and Benin with a great deal of material on the Vili and on fetishism. Dennett also includes a few highly regarded notes on the language of the Vili. The illustrations included in this work are

unique. Appendices include extracts from Bishop James Johnson's 'Yoruba Heathenism' and Professor J. A. Abayomi Cole's 'Astrological Geomancy in Africa'.

131 **Die Babinga Pygmaen.** (The Babinga pygmies.)
Wilhelm Dupré. *Annali de Pontificio Museo Missionario Etnologica*, vol. 26 (1962), p. 9-172.

Compiled by missionaries, this German-language work is the longest of the few studies of the Congo's pygmy groups.

132 **Catastrophe and creation: the transformation of an African culture.**
Kajsa E. Friedman. Chur, Switzerland; Philadelphia, Pennsylvania: Harwood, 1991. 271p. map. bibliog.

Drawing on a wealth of anthropological and historical material, Friedman's recent study of the Bakongo looks at the transformations which took place within the group as a result of the slave trade and colonization.

133 **Les Babinga des rives de l'Oubangui.** (The Babinga on the banks of the Ubangui.)
G. Grangeion. *Afrique et Asie*, vol. 71 (1965), p. 34-42.

The pygmies of the northern Congo are the subject of this short article in French.

134 **Les Babingas.** (The Babingas.)
André Hauser. *Zaïre*, vol. 7 (Feb. 1953), p. 146-79.

Hauser provides a good overview of the Babinga pygmies in this short article in French.

135 **The Fang.**
Human Relations Area Files. New Haven, Connecticut: HRAF, 1960. 49 microfiches. maps.

This microfilm collection includes ethnological information on the Fang and numerous other African groups as well as appropriate maps and illustrations.

136 **Congo crosses, a study of Congo womanhood.**
Julia Lake Kellersberger. Boston, Massachusetts: The Central Committee on the United Study of Foreign Missions, 1936. 222p. maps.

This illustrated study of women and women's issues among the Bakongo also includes material on the group's wider social life and customs. The position of women in Congolese society was traditionally that of mothers and tillers of the soil. Christian missions, French colonial administrators, Congolese governments and political parties have all sought to enhance the status of women. Indeed many urban women lead very different lives from those of their rural sisters who remain in a world of heavy labour, polygamy, arbitrary divorce and inflated bride-prices. Although great strides have been taken in the education of girls, little of the Congolese governments' years of revolutionary rhetoric has had an effect on the lives of women.

137 **The Kongo.**
Karl Laman.   Uppsala, Sweden: Institutionem för Allmän och
Jämförande Etnografi vid Uppsala Universitet, 1953, 1957, 1962, 1968.
4 vols. (Studia Ethnographica Upsaliensia).
Laman's extensive work on the Bakongo is the largest and most detailed ethnography
of the group in English.

138 **L'Initiation Bakongo et sa signification.** (Bakongo initiation and its
significance.)
Ferdinand Ngoma.   Lubumbashi, Zaïre: Centre d'Etudes de
Problemes Sociaux Indigènes, 1965. 196p. map.
Ngoma's study of Bakongo beliefs is a rewritten treatment of his 1963 doctoral thesis at
the Sorbonne. Initiation ceremonies for boys include circumcision. Girls participate in
tchikumbi, which is a combined engagement and coming of age ceremony
characterized by body painting, wearing jewellery and dancing. As in many equatorial
African rituals, symbolism reaffirms connections in lineage. Herbs, amulets and sacred
baskets of relics known as *nkobi alubaku* also feature in many of these rites.

139 **La cuvette Congolaise: les hommes et les structures.** (The Congo basin:
the people and structures.)
Theophile Obenga.   Paris: Présence Africaine, 1976. 172p.
This account of the cultures of the Congo basin concentrates on the author's own
M'Boshi tribe, which lives in the north of the Congo. Seventeen pages of illustrations
accompany this text.

140 **Elements de base pour une approche ethnologique et historique des
Fang-Beti-Boulou.** (Basic elements for an ethnological and historical
approach to the Fang-Beti-Boulou.)
Jean-Pierre Ombolo.   Yaoundé, Cameroon: University of Yaoundé,
1984. 308p. maps.
Unlike most studies of the Fang in which the viewpoint is colonial, Gabonese or Río
Munian, Professor Ombolo of the University of Yaoundé discusses the Fang and the
related Beti and Boulou from a Cameroonian stance. Such a viewpoint is valuable and
relevant to studies of the Congolese Fang given the intense cross-border trade and
migration of the group. Using numerous drawings and other illustrations, Ombolo is
able to provide much material on the Fang and their society, language, religion,
systems of authority, music, crafts, genealogy, masks, weapons, family systems and
relationships with neighbouring groups.

141 **Les populations Batéké.** (The Bateke people.)
Louis Papy.   *Cahiers d'Outre-Mer*, vol. 2, no. 2 (April-June 1949),
p. 112-34.
This short and dated article in French remains one of the best introductions to the
Bateke of the Congo.

142 **La circoncisión Bakota.** (Bakota circumcision.)
Louis Perrois. *Cahiers de l'Office de la Recherche Scientifique et Technique d'Outre-Mer (Série Sciences Humaines)*, vol. 5, no. 1 (Jan. 1968), p. 1-109.
This lengthy French-language article is one of a very few works on the customs of Bakota tribe, which inhabits the Congo and Gabon.

143 **Articulation des modes de dépendances et des modes de réproduction dans deux sociétés lignagères.** (An explanation of the modes of dependence and reproduction in two lineage societies.)
Pierre Philippe Rey. *Cahiers d'Etudes Africaines*, vol. 9, no. 3 (1969), p. 415-40.
The social orders of the Punu and Kunyi, two small, isolated ethnic groups of the Congo, are the subjects of this article.

144 **Les Kongo nord occidentaux.** (The northwestern Bakongo.)
Marcel Soret. Paris: Presses Universitaires de France, 1959. 144p. bibliog.
Accompanied by illustrations and a bibliography, Soret's well-researched French-language book is an ethnology and history of Loango and neighbouring states.

145 **Les Batéké Balali.** (The Balali Bateke.)
Edouard Trezenem. *Journal de la Société des Africanistes*, (Paris), vol. 10 (1940), p. 1-62.
The Bateke of the central Congo are the topic of this good introductory article.

146 **Introduction à l'ethnographie du Congo.** (Introduction to the ethnography of the Congo.)
Jan Vansina. Kinshasa, Zaïre: Université Lovanium; Brussels: CRISP, 1965. 228p. maps. bibliog.
This is the most comprehensive work on the peoples of modern-day Zaïre, some of whom, such as the Bakongo and Bateke, are also found in the Congo. Maps and a bibliography are included.

147 **Kingdoms of the savanna.**
Jan Vansina. Madison, Wisconsin: University of Wisconsin, 1966. 364p. bibliog.
This is one of several works by ethnologist and historian Jan Vansina which looks at the peoples and states of equatorial Africa. Focusing on the Teke Kingdom, his discussion of the extreme decentralization of the area (p. 102-10) is particularly interesting. This account of the Bateke and their past is based on collected oral traditions. His bibliography offers numerous important and unique sources. Vansina's research leading up to this work includes the previous item and also 'Noms personnels et structure social chez les Tyo' (Personal names and social structures among the Bateke) in *Bulletin des Séances*, (Brussels), vol. 4 (1964), p. 794-804 and 'Research

among the Tyo of Congo Brazzaville' *Africa*, (London), vol. 34, no. 4 (Oct.-Dec. 1964), p. 375.

148 **Etudes Bakongo.** (Bakongo studies.)
     J. van Wing.   Bruges, Belgium: Desclée-De Brouwer, 1959. 512p.

Bakongo ethnology, sociology, religion and magic are examined in great detail in this illustrated French-language reference work, which is a combined edition of *Etudes Bakongo I* (1921. 319p.) which dealt with the group's history and sociology; and *Etudes Bakongo II* (1938. 301p.) which confined itself to religion and magic.

Area handbook for the People's Republic of the Congo (Congo Brazzaville).
See item no. 3.

The country of the dwarfs.
See item no. 13.

A journey to Ashango-land and further penetration into equatorial Africa.
See item no. 14.

Wild bush tribes of tropical Africa.
See item no. 16.

Travels in West Africa: Congo Français, Corisco and Cameroons.
See item no. 20.

De l'Atlantique au fleuve Congo: une géographie du souspeuplement. (From the Atlantic to the Congo: a geography of underpopulation.)
See item no. 38.

The native problem in Africa.
See item no. 71.

Daily life in the Kingdom of the Kongo: from the sixteenth to the eighteenth century.
See item no. 92.

L'Ancien royaume de Congo. (The old kingdom of the Congo.)
See item no. 93.

The Kingdom of the Kongo.
See item no. 95.

The rise of Congolese state systems.
See item no. 96.

The history of Loango, Kakongo and other kingdoms in Africa.
See item no. 97.

L'Ancien royaume du Congo des origines à la fin du XIXe siècle. (The old kingdom of the Congo from its origins to the end of the nineteenth century.)
See item no. 98.

The dark kingdoms: the impact of white civilization on three great African monarchies.
See item no. 99.

The Kingdom of Kongo.
See item no. 100.

George Grenfell and the Congo.
See item no. 104.

The Tio Kingdom of the middle Congo: 1880-1892.
See item no. 110.

Messianic popular movements in the lower Congo.
See item no. 171.

Messianismes et nationalismes en Afrique noire. (Messianic movements and nationalisms in black Africa.)
See item no. 173.

Drugs and mysticism: the Bwiti of the Fang.
See item no. 174.

Le Harrisme et le Bwiti: deux réactions Africaines à l'impact Chrétien. (Harrism and the Bwiti: two African reactions to the impact of Christianity.)
See item no. 175.

Kimbanguism, prophetic Christianity in the Congo.
See item no. 177.

Bwiti: an ethnography of the religious imagination in Africa.
See item no. 178.

Red-white-black as a mode of thought.
See item no. 179.

An anthology of Kongo religion: primary texts from lower Zaïre.
See item no. 180.

The cultural roots of Kongo prophetism.
See item no. 181.

Modern Kongo prophets: religion in a plural society.
See item no. 182.

La naissance a l'envers: essai sur le rituel du Bwiti Fang au Gabon. (Birth on the wrong side: an essay on the Bwiti Fang ritual of Gabon.)
See item no. 184.

Le messianisme Congolais et ses incidences politiques. (Congolese messianism and its political effects.)
See item no. 186.

Litterature traditionnelle des M'bochi. (Traditional literature of the M'boshi.)
See item no. 431.

Ethnic Groups

Proverbes Kongo. (Kongo proverbs.)
See item no. 436.

Les proverbes anciens du Bas-Congo. (The old proverbs of the lower Congo.)
See item no. 454.

Notes sur la musique des Bochiman comparée à celle des Pygmees Babinga.
(Notes on the music of the Bushmen compared to that of the Babinga
pygmies.)
See item no. 468.

Cahiers d'Outre-mer. (Overseas notes.)
See item no. 517.

Encyclopédie coloniale et maritime, volume V. (Colonial and maritime
encyclopedia, volume five.)
See item no. 519.

Encyclopédie mensuelle d'outre-mer. (The monthly overseas encyclopaedia.)
See item no. 520.

Languages

149 Dialectes du Gabon: la famille des langues Téké. (Gabonese dialects: the Teke language family.)
J. J. Adams. *Bulletin de l'Institut d'Etudes Centrafricaines*, vol. 1, no. 7-8 (1954), p. 33-107.
The language of the Bateke tribe is examined in this French language article on the group's dialects in Gabon.

150 Dictionary and grammar of the Kongo language.
William Holman Bentley. London: Baptist Missionary Society, 1887. 719p.
This reference on Kikongo by an English missionary continues to be of importance in understanding the language of this important group which extends from the Congo, south through Zaïre and Angola. It was also reprinted in Farnborough, New Jersey by Gregg in 1967.

151 English-Congo and Congo-English dictionary.
Henry Craven, John Barfield. Freeport, New York: Books for Libraries Press, 1971. 248p.
First published in 1883, this work is one of the oldest of its kind and is the definitive English reference work. This reprint is part of the Black Heritage Library Collection.

152 Language map of Africa and the adjacent islands.
David Dalby. London: International African Institute, 1977. 63p.
The areas in which the various languages of the Congo are spoken is clarified and explained in this booklet which accompanies a linguistic map of Africa.

Languages

153 **English-Lingala dictionary.**
John Ellington. Kinshasa: J. Ellington, 1982. 150p.
This is the most recent English-language dictionary of Lingala, an important trade
language of the northern Congo, Zaïre and southern Central African Republic.

154 **Le Lingala, parle et ecrit.** (Lingala, spoken and written.)
Nestor van Everroeck. Antwerp, Belgium: Standaard-Boek Handel,
1969. 206p.
A French-language textbook of Lingala grammar with exercises.

155 **The origins and development of Kituba.**
Harold W. Fehderau. Kisangani, Congo-Leopoldville (Zaïre):
Universite Libre en Congo, 1967. 124p. bibliog.
This study of Kituba, a trade language similar to Kikongo, arises from the author's
PhD thesis at Cornell University, Ithaca, New York. As the lingua franca of the
southern Congo, southwestern Zaïre and northern Angola, this language has both
historical and current importance.

156 **Sango: rundfunk und zeitungstexte.** (Sangha: broadcast and newspaper
texts.)
Luc Feidangai. Saarbrucken, Germany: Institut fur Phonetik,
Universitat des Saarlandes, 1986. 69p.
One of the most recent materials to be published on the language of the Sangha, this
book is a short collection of press extracts in Sangha with German translations.

157 **Dictionnaire Fang-Français et Français-Fang.** (A Fang-French and
French-Fang dictionary.)
Samuel Galley. Neuchâtel, Switzerland: Henri Messeitler, 1964. 588p.
This is the only comprehensive dictionary translating Fang into a major European
language.

158 **The Bantu languages of western equatorial Africa.**
Malcolm Guthrie. London: International African Institute, 1953. 94p.
As part of this general survey of languages, Guthrie has included material on the many
languages of the Congo.

159 **Lingala grammar and dictionary.**
Malcolm Guthrie. London: Baptist Missionary Society, 1988. 238p.
This revised edition of Guthrie's 1935 original (Leopoldville-Ouest, Belgian Congo:
Conseil Protestant du Congo) is considered the best textbook of this important trading
language.

160 **Dictionnaire Kikongo-Français.** (A Kikongo-French dictionary.)
   Karl E. Laman.   Ridgewood, New Jersey: Gregg, 1964. 2 vols.
Originally published in Brussels in 1936, this Kikongo dictionary is the most comprehensive in a major European language. Bibliographical references are included in an introduction. A folding map of the Kikongo region is also provided.

161 **Vocabulaire Kikongo-Français.** (A Kikongo-French vocabulary.)
   K. E. Laman, M. Westling.   Kinshasa, Zaïre: Eglise Evangelique du Congo, 1972. 59p.
An abridged dictionary of Kikongo drawn from item no. 160.

162 **Dictionnaire Français-Ngbandi, Ngbandi-Français.** (A French-Ubangi, Ubangi-French dictionary.)
   Benjamin Lekens.   Turvuren, Belgium: Musée Royal de l'Afrique Centrale, 1952. 348p.
The Ngbandi (or Gbandi) language of the Central African Republic and northern Zaïre is closely related to Bonole and Ikasa, two minor languages of the northern Congo. Known in the English-speaking world as the Ubangi, the speakers of this language were also significant within the framework of French Equatorial Africa.

163 **Vocabulaire Lingala-Français, Français-Lingala.** (Lingala-French, French-Lingala vocabulary.)
   Missionnaires de Scheut a Nouvel-Anvers.   Turnhout, Belgium: Etablissements H. Proost & Cie., [n.d.]. 344p.
This dictionary, produced by Belgian missionaries in Zaïre, remains one of the best reference works on Lingala in a major European language.

164 **English-Lingala manual.**
   John D. Odhner.   Washington, DC: University Press of America, 1981. 187p.
A recent grammar of Lingala in English.

165 **Lexique Français-Ikota.** (A French-Ikota lexicon.)
   R. P. Perrou.   Makoukou, Gabon: Mission Catholique, 1964. 2 vols.
The language of the Bakota people is the subject of this dictionary in French.

166 **Cultural languages and contact vernaculars in the Republic of the Congo.**
   E. Polome.   *Texas Studies in Literature and Language*, vol. 4, no. 4 (Winter 1963), p. 499-511.
The usage of ethnic languages, such as Kikongo, Sangha and Fang, and of trade languages, such as Kituba and Lingala, is examined in this short article on language in the Congo.

Languages

167 A grammar of Sango.
William J. Samarin. The Hague, Netherlands: Mouton, 1967. 284p.

A study of Sangha grammar in English, Samarin also wrote a similar text in French: *Sango: Langue de l'Afrique Centrale* (Leiden: Brill, 1970). A map of the Sangha region of the northern Congo is included.

168 The structure of Sango narrative.
Charles R. Taber. Hartford, Connecticut: Hartford Seminary Foundation, 1966. 2 vols. bibliog.

A study of the Sangha language, which is spoken in the Congo, Cameroon and the Central African Republic. This look at Sangha language and oral literature would be of use to both scholars of African literature and those wishing to learn Sangha.

169 Lingala: basic course.
J. Redden, F. Bongo, (et al.). Washington, DC: Foreign Service Institute, 1963. 293p.

Sponsored by the United States Department of State, this course in Lingala is useful in acquiring a basic grasp of the language.

170 Benue-Congo comparative wordlist.
Edited by Kay Williamson, Kiyoshi Shimizu. Ibadan, Nigeria: West African Linguistic Society (University of Ibadan Press), 1968. [n.p.].

This series of glossaries of Benue-Congo languages of the Bantu family was compiled by the Benue-Congo Working Group at the University of Ibadan's West African Linguistic Society. It is useful in comparing the vocabularies of various tongues in order to determine historical, cultural and linguistic relationships and linkages within this under-studied language community, which had no tradition of literacy before colonialism. With the exception of the Babinga and several other very small groups in the north, almost all of the languages of the Congo are of this grouping.

Proverbes Kongo. (Kongo proverbs.)
See item no. 436.

Les proverbes anciens du Bas-Congo. (The old proverbs of the lower Congo.)
See item no. 454.

Bulletin de l'Institut de Recherches Scientifiques au Congo. (Bulletin of the Institute for Scientific Research in the Congo.)
See item no. 515.

Religion and Philosophy

Traditional African

171 **Messianic popular movements in the lower Congo.**
Efraim Andersson. Uppsala, Sweden: Almqvist & Wiksell; New York: W. S. Heinman, 1958. 287p.
The rise of messianic movements combining religious syncreticism with liberation politics has been one of the most important social transformations in equatorial Africa in the twentieth century. Complete with illustrations, this work traces the pre-independence growth of movements led by Simon Kimbangu, André Matswa and others.

172 **Matswa.**
Anonymous. *Monde-Non-Chrétien* (Paris), vol. 7, no. 26 (June 1953), p. 202-10.
Written a decade after his death in 1942, this short French-language article on Matswa is a good introduction to this mystical figure regarded as a prophet by the Lari branch of the Bakongo.

173 **Messianismes et nationalismes en Afrique noire.** (Messianic movements and nationalisms in black Africa.)
Georges Balandier. *Cahiers Internationaux de Sociologie* (Paris), vol. 14 (1953), p. 41-65.
Balandier's article examines the connections between religious syncreticism and political nationalism throughout Africa during the first half of the twentieth century. The movements founded by Kimbangu and Matswa feature prominently.

174 **Drugs and mysticism: the Bwiti of the Fang.**
Jacques Binet. *Diogènes* (Paris), vol. 86. (Summer 1974), p. 31-54.
This article highlights the use of marijuana and the hallucinogen iboga in Bwiti (Fang)
rituals similar to Christian communion.

175 **Le Harrisme et le Bwiti: deux réactions Africaines à l'impact Chrétien.**
(Harrisism and the Bwiti: two African reactions to the impact of
Christianity.)
René Bureau. *Recherches de Sciences Religieuses*, vol. 63, no. 1
(Jan.–March 1975), p. 83-100.
This comparison of religious syncreticism in Africa looks at Harrisism in west Africa
and the Bwiti cult among the Fang of Gabon, the Congo, Cameroon and Río Muni.

176 **La passion de Simon Kimbangu.** (The passion of Simon Kimbangu.)
Jules Chomé. Brussels: Les Amis de Présence Africaine, 1959. 131p.
Simon Kimbangu (1889-1951) founded the largest of central Africa's syncretic sects
derived from Christianity. This biographical work concentrates on his last thirty years
when he had turned himself over to the colonial authorities in the Belgian Congo.
Kimbangu's life and teachings inspired André Matswa, Zepherin Lassy, Fulbert
Youlou and others in the French Congo.

177 **Kimbanguism, prophetic Christianity in the Congo.**
Harold W. Fehderau. *Practical Anthropology*, vol. 9, no. 4 (July-
Aug. 1962), p. 157-78.
Although concentrating on the former Belgian Congo, this article describes a religious
movement which was both directly influential in the Congo and the prototype of
similar groups in French Equatorial Africa.

178 **Bwiti: an ethnography of the religious imagination in Africa.**
James W. Fernandez. Princeton, New Jersey: Princeton University
Press, 1982. 731p. bibliog.
This excellent detailed work on the religious beliefs and practices of the Fang is the
result of years of experience and painstaking research on the part of Fernandez.
Although most of his research was conducted in Gabon, some information is included
on the Congo. There are chapters on Fang-European contacts, beliefs regarding space,
time and the past, resource distribution, sexual relations, authority, initiation rites, the
occult, ritual, morality, religious architecture, liturgy, music, dreams, visions, morality,
linguistics and healing. Three useful appendicies include a glossary of terms, texts of
Bwiti sermons and information on Mbiri societies. The numerous illustrations and
photographs throughout the book are the work of Fernandez and his wife, Renate.

179 **Red-white-black as a mode of thought.**
Anita Jacobson-Widding. Uppsala, Sweden: Almquist & Wiksell,
1979. 396p. bibliog.
Subtitled 'a study of triadic classification by colours in the ritual symbolism and
cognitive thought of the peoples of the lower Congo', this detailed, illustrated
anthropological and philosophical work examines the tri-polar thought patterns of the

Bakongo in which rather than viewing ideas as dichotomies, the concept of a third, neutral 'pole' is important.

180 **An anthology of Kongo religion: primary texts from lower Zaïre.**
   J. M. Janzen, W. MacGaffey.   Lawrence, Kansas: University of
   Kansas, 1974. 163p.
This collection of traditional animist, Kimbangist and other religious writings is accompanied by explanatory notes, a short bibliography and a map.

181 **The cultural roots of Kongo prophetism.**
   Wyatt MacGaffey.   *History of Religions*, vol. 17, no. 2 (Nov. 1977),
   p. 177-93.
This article examines the cultural and social contexts of messianism among the Bakongo in the Congo and Zaïre.

182 **Modern Kongo prophets: religion in a plural society.**
   Wyatt MacGaffey.   Bloomington, Indiana: University of Indiana
   Press, 1983. 285p. bibliog. (African Systems of Thought Series.)
MacGaffey analyses the degree to which 20th century religious experience among the Bakongo has been syncretic.

183 **Religion and society in central Africa.**
   Wyatt MacGaffey.   Chicago, Illinois: University of Chicago Press,
   1986. 295p. bibliog.
MacGaffey examines the beliefs of the Bakongo in this recent study of the lower Congo.

184 **La naissance a l'envers: essai sur le rituel du Bwiti Fang au Gabon.**
   (Birth on the wrong side: an essay on the Bwiti Fang ritual of Gabon.)
   André Mary.   Paris: L'Harmattan, 1983. 384p. bibliog.
Concentrating on the artistic, mystical and literary side of Fang traditional religion, Mary's study of Gabonese Bwiti ritual is equally relevant to the northern Congo.

185 **Simon Kimbangu, prophete et martyr Zaïrois.** (Simon Kimbangu,
   Zaïrean prophet and martyr.)
   Martial Sinda.   Paris: ABC; Dakar: Nouvelles Éditions Africaines,
   1977. 111p. map.
This biography of Congolese messianic leader Kimbangu (1889-1951) is uncritical and adulatory. It was written by a Congolese (Brazzaville) writer who has produced several similar works.

186 **Le messianisme Congolais et ses incidences politiques.** (Congolese messianism and its political effects.)
Martial Sinda.   Paris: Payot, 1972. 390p.
This French-language history of Kimbanguism, Matswaism and other nativistic politico-religious movements was compiled by Congolese writer Sinda.

187 **Le Matsouanisme.** (Matswanism.)
Fulbert Youlou.   Brazzaville: Imprimerie Centrale, 1955. various paginations.
Fulbert Youlou, first President of the Congo, climbed to the top of his country's political system largely because of his claims to have been the spiritual (and political) successor to André Matswa. In this short book, written early in his career, he lays out his claims, defines Matswanism and maps out the movement's future. Corruption, unpopular policies and blatant favouritism for his Lari followers led to his downfall in the summer of 1963.

André Matsoua: fondateur du mouvement de liberation du Congo. (André Matswa: founder of the Congo's liberation movement.)
See item no. 509.
Cahiers d'études Africaines. (African studies notes.)
See item no. 516.
Encyclopédie mensuelle d'outre-mer. (The monthly overseas encyclopaedia.)
See item no. 520.

General Christian

188 **Churches at the grass-roots: study in Congo-Brazzaville.**
Efraim Andersson.   London: Lutterworth, 1968. 296p. bibliog.
This excellent history of Christian missions and churches in the Congo, though somewhat dated is a valuable and useful presentation of its field of study. Andersson is one of the leading authorities on religion in the Congo.

189 **The churches of equatorial Africa.**
Jean Keller.   *Practical Anthropology*, vol. 10, no. 1 (Jan.-Feb. 1963), p. 16-21.
A general overview of Christianity in the Congo at the time of independence is provided in this article.

Roman Catholicism

190 **Annuaire de l'Eglise Catholique en Afrique Francophone (Missions Catholiques), 1978-79.** (Annual of the Catholic Church in Francophone Africa [Catholic missions], 1978-79.)
Anonymous. Paris: ONPC-RF, 1978. 688p.
This detailed reference work provides a good description of the Roman Catholic Church and its activities in Francophone Africa since independence.

191 **L'Eglise Catholique et l'etat Congo de 1960 à nos jours.** (The Catholic Church and the Congolese state from 1960 to the present.)
S. M. Makosso. *Afrique Contemporaine*, vol. 15, no. 6 (Nov.-Dec. 1976).
The contemporary history of the Roman Catholic Church in the Congo is the subject of this article, one of a very few on this topic since independence.

192 **Missions d'Afrique: le Congo Français, le Gabon.** (African missions: the French Congo, Gabon.)
Alexandre le Roy. In: *Les Missions Catholiques Françaises au XIXe Siècle.* Edited by J. B. Piolet Paris: Armand Colin, 1902, vol. 5. p. 219-54.
Vicar Apostolic of Gabon from 1892 to 1896, Father Alexandre le Roy was famous for his advocacy of the use of vernacular languages in African religious education. While Superior General of the Holy Ghost Fathers he wrote several influential works concerning the Congo and Gabon. Among them are writings on pygmies and Gabonese ethnic groups, as well as this excellent contribution to mission history.

Adventures and observations on the west coast of Africa and its islands.
See item no. 27.

La Semaine. (The Week.)
See item no. 495.

Protestantism

193 **The environment, establishment and development of Protestant missions in French Equatorial Africa.**
Benjamin A. Hamilton. Unpublished PhD thesis, Grace Theological Seminary, Goshen, Indiana, 1959. 352p.
This is by far the best work on Protestantism in French Equatorial Africa. More recent information is difficult to obtain, but may be gleaned from short articles in Baptist, Salvation Army, Jehovah Witness and other denominational publications.

Religion and Philosophy

George Grenfell and the Congo.
See item no. 105.

Social Conditions

194 Sociologie des Brazzaville noires. (Sociology of Brazzaville blacks.)
Georges Balandier. Paris: Presses de la Fondation National des
Sciences Politiques, 1985. 306p.

Augmented by Jean Copans, this is a revised edition of Balandier's 1955 original
(Paris: Librarie Colin). The work of an eminent French sociologist, this is an excellent
portrayal of Brazzaville society.

195 Ambiguous Africa.
Georges Balandier. New York: Pantheon, 1966. 276p.

An English translation of Balandier's 1957 French original, *Afrique Ambigue* (Paris:
Plon) by Helen Weaver, this sociological work includes much material on conditions in
Brazzaville.

196 The sociology of black Africa.
Georges Balandier. London: Andre Deutsch, 1970. 540p.

This general work on the sociology of the African continent is particularly strong in
explaining the impact of colonialization and Western influence on African societies in
the Congo and Gabon, Balandier's favourite subjects of study. This work is a
translation of the author's 1963 French original *Sociologie Actuelle de l'Afrique Noire*
(Paris: Presses Universitaires de France).

**197 Jeune Afrique mobilisable: les problèmes de la jeunesse désoeurvrée en
Afrique noire.** (Workable young Africa: the problems of unemployed
youth in black Africa.)
Georges Edouard Bourgoignie. Paris: Éditions Universitaires, 1964.
213p.

The problem of youth unemployment has continued to be particularly serious in the
Congo, which is featured in this article written during the early days of Massamba-
Débat's regime.

198 **Les femmes au Congo.** (Women in the Congo.)
Charles J. Castellani. Paris: Éditions Flammarion, 1898. 307p.
Castellani's study of the women of the southern French Congo is unique for its time. This work is available on microfilm, produced by Research Publications (New Haven, Connecticut: 1976), as number 3950 in the *History of Women* series.

199 **Les enfants de Poto-Poto.** (The children of Poto-Poto.)
Michel Croce-Spinelli. Paris: Grasset, 1967. 367p.
The customs and social and economic conditions of Brazzaville's poor are examined in this French sociological work, which is important not only as a study of Third World hardship and unemployment, but also as an examination of the urban realities of a continent often mistakenly viewed by Westerners as being rural and traditionalist.

200 **Le Chômage à Brazzaville: etude sociologique.** (Unemployment in Brazzaville: a sociological study.)
Roland Devauges. Paris: ORSTOM, 1963. 2 vols.
Compiled from research conducted in 1957, this study of the Congolese capital predicted the difficulties which lay ahead when the forces of unemployment, a youthful population and politicization would be unleashed following independence. A more condensed look at Devauges' research is provided by his *Les Chomeurs de Brazzaville et les Perspectives du Barrage du Kouilou* (The unemployed of Brazzaville and perspectives on the Kouilou Dam – Paris: ORSTOM, 1963), a 100-page book which surveys labour in Brazzaville and Pointe-Noire and the potential of the proposed Kouilou Dam.

201 **The white man as seen through the eyes of Congolese (Brazzaville) children.**
Pierre Erny. *US Joint Publications Research Service Translations on Africa* (Washington, DC), no. 475 (1966), p. 1-12.
This illuminating and unusual psychological study is a translation of Erny's article in *Psychologie des Peuples* (Paris) vol. 21 (July-Sept. 1966), p. 365-75.

202 **Women in Brazzaville-Congo.**
Jeanne-Françoise Vencent. *Women Today* (London), vol. 6, no. 5 (Dec. 1965), p. 116.
Congolese women have traditionally been expected to be fertile, industrious, poised and capable of managing a household. Their treatment ranges from a high status as matriarchs within traditional matrilineal societies to virtual subjugation in others. The status of Congolese women is examined in this short, translated article by a French writer.

A survey of political, economic and sociological development in the Congo (Brazzaville).
See item no. 2.

The native problem in Africa.
See item no. 71.

Histoire et sociologie politiques du Congo. (A history and political sociology of the Congo.)
See item no. 117.

Inter-African Labour Institute Bulletin.
See item no. 372.

Bulletin de l'Institut de Recherches Scientifiques au Congo. (Bulletin of the Institute for Scientific Research in the Congo.)
See item no. 515.

Encyclopedia of the Third World.
See item no. 523.

Health

203 **A kit for in vitro isolation of trypanosomes in the field: first trial with sleeping sickness patients in the Congo Republic.**
D. Aerts, P. Truc, L. Penchenier. *Transactions of the Royal Society of Tropical Medicine*, vol. 86, no. 4 (July 1992), p. 394.
The rapid and easily available diagnosis of sleeping sickness is the goal of this recent study.

204 **The spread of HIV-1 in Africa: sexual contact patterns and the predicted demographic impact of AIDS.**
C. Anderson, R. M. May, (et al.). *Nature*, vol. 352, no. 6336 (15 Aug. 1991), p. 581-890.
This article, which takes the form of a discussion, examines HIV-1 and AIDS infections in Africa, the epidemiology of AIDS, sexual behaviour and various mathematical projections for the future.

205 **Community health achievements in Africa.**
Anonymous. *The Lancet*, vol. 340, no. 8825 (17 Nov. 1992), p. 967.
A brief news item in this medical journal notes the first International Conference on Community Health in Africa, held in Brazzaville in September 1992. The conference concerned itself with health promotion, disease control, community mobilization, the participation of traditional healers in AIDS prevention and other related topics.

206 **Sleeping sickness.**
Anonymous. *Science*, vol. 105, no. 47 (23 Nov. 1984), p. 956-9.
Disseminated by the tsetse fly, trypanosomiasis or African sleeping sickness is a disease which has defied vaccination because of the complicated ways in which it foils the immune system. As trypanosomiasis research increases, biologists are fascinated by the genetic mechanisms used by the parasites that cause this disease. An inset with this

excellent article questions whether there is a connection between African sleeping sickness and AIDS.

207 **Schistosomes, development, reproduction and host relations.**
Paul F. Basch. New York, Oxford: Oxford University Press, 1991.
248p. bibliog.
This illustrated study is one of the most comprehensive references to schistosomes and schistosomiasis (bilharzia). A lengthy bibliography is provided.

208 **Current practices for the prevention and treatment of malaria in children and in pregnant women in the Brazzaville region.**
B. Carme, P. Koulengana, A. Nzambi. *Annales of Tropical Medicine and Parasitology*, vol. 86, no. 4 (1 Aug. 1992), p. 319-50.
The intention of this article is to provide insights into practices for preventing and treating malaria with a view towards future improvement.

209 **Malaria in Africa.**
Michael Colbourne. London: Oxford University Press, 1966. 115p.
Maps, tables and diagrams accompany this short book, which is a good introduction to malaria, its range, effects, treatment and prevention.

210 **Enquete nutritionnelle en Republique du Congo: resultats de enquete nationale realisée en 1987.** (A nutritional survey of the Republic of the Congo: results of the national survey conducted in 1987.)
A. Cornu, F. Delpeuch, F. Simondon. *Bulletin of the World Health Organization*, vol. 69, no. 5 (Sept.-Oct. 1991), p. 561-9.
This is a short piece reviewing the results of a far-reaching national nutritional survey in the Congo.

211 **The role of cassava in the etiology of endemic goiter and cretinism.**
A. M. Ermans, (et al.). Ottawa: International Development Research Centre, 1980. 182p. bibliog.
This illustrated study examines the relationship between a cassava-dominated diet and hypothyroidism in the Congo. A medically useful bibliography is included.

212 **African perceptions of AIDS: another way of dying.**
Bruce E. Fleming. *The Nation*, vol. 250, no. 13 (2 April 1990), p. 446-9.
Although not primarily about the Congo, this article is important in describing the fatalism and helplessness with which AIDS is viewed in Africa. It provides a view of the disease which is very different than those evident in the developed world. In the Congo, AIDS is particularly prominent in Pointe-Noire (between six and eight per cent adult infection rate) and Brazzaville (four per cent adult infection rate).

213 **Observations on the fevers of the west coast of Africa.**
Henry A. Ford. New York: Edward Jenkins, 1856. 48p.

This early work on diseases in the humid regions of tropical Africa's Atlantic coast
provides not only information on the 'fevers' for scholars and travellers of the day, but
also material on early attitudes regarding health in the tropics.

214 **A clinical study of intestinal bilharziosis (Schistosoma Mansomi) in
Africa.**
Michael Gelfand. London: Arnold, 1967. 230p.

A good introductory account of schistosomiasis, a major debilitating disease of tropical
Africa is provided in this medical work on the disease's treatment.

215 **How AIDS forces reappraisal of hepatitis B virus control in sub-Saharan
Africa.**
C. P. Hudson. *Lancet*, vol. 336, no. 8727 (1 Dec. 1990), p. 1364-7.

Hudson suggests that AIDS prevention programmes should be used to educate
Africans about how to avoid hepatitis as well as HIV infection. Information on
vaccination strategies and on the transmission and impact of AIDS is also provided.

216 **International journal for vitamin and nutrition research.**
New York: 1930- . [n.p.], quarterly.

Throughout 1990 this journal published the results of several vitamin and nutritional
studies on Congolese children. Number 2 (April-June) featured vitamin E research on
rural children by M. D. Laryea, E. Mayatepek and P. Brunninger and numbers 3 and
4 (July-Sept. & Oct.-Dec.) compared vitamin A deficiency and malarial attack in pre-
school children studied by P. Galan, R. Luzeau and C. Sambra.

217 **Nutritional factors involved in the goitrogenic action of cassava.**
Edited by F. B. Iteke, A. M. Ermans, F. Delange. Ottawa:
International Development Research Centre, 1982. 100p.

Additional findings on thyroid conditions and cassava consumption are found in this
work which builds on item no. 211.

218 **Characteristics associated with HIV-1 infection in pregnant women in
Brazzaville, Congo.**
M. Lallemant, S. Lallemant-Le Coeur, D. Cheynier. *Journal of
Acquired Immune Deficiency Syndrome*, vol. 5, no. 3 (March 1992),
p. 279.

Although severely affected by the AIDS epidemic sweeping the African continent, the
Congo has not been an area of widespread research, as have Zaïre, Rwanda, Burundi
and Uganda. This is the most recent of the very few articles on AIDS which have been
specific to the Congo.

219 The ecology of malnutrition in middle Africa: Ghana, Nigeria, Republic of the Congo, Rwanda, Burundi and the former French Equatorial Africa.
Jacques M. May. New York: Hafner, 1965. 255p. maps. bibliog.
As an analysis of food supply, diet and malnutrition in selected tropical African countries, including the Congo, this work was part of the publisher's series on medical geography and food geography, both of which were sponsored by the US Army Natick Laboratories under contract DA19-129-QM-1946(N).

220 Population dynamics of Loa loa and Mansonella perstans infections in individuals living in an endemic area of the Congo.
F. Noireau, G. Pichon. *The American Journal of Tropical Medicine and Hygiene*, vol. 46, no. 6 (June 1992), p. 672.
François Noireau, a leading expert on the parasitic diseases of the western Congo basin co-authored this study of two leading parasitic infections in the Congo. His earlier articles have included one on Loa loa transmission in the Chaillu mountains in *The American Journal of Tropical Medicine and Hygiene*, vol. 43, no. 3 (Sept. 1990), and the epidemiology of Mansonella perstans, *Annals of Tropical Medicine and Parasitology*, vol. 84, no. 3 (June 1990).

221 Infestation by Auchmeromyia senegalensis as a consequence of the adoption of non-nomadic life by pygmies in the Congo Republic.
François Noireau. *Transactions of the Royal Society of Tropical Medicine*, vol. 86, no. 3 (May 1992), p. 329.
In this highly interesting, recent article, Noireau examines the medical results of the Babinga pygmies' increasing abandonment of their nomadic lifestyle.

222 Epidemiologie et prophylaxie des endemies dominantes en Afrique noire. (An epidemiology and prophylaxis of the major endemic diseases in black Africa.)
Edited by M. Payet, M. Sankale. Paris: Masson et Cie., 1968. 224p.
This text on the principal communicable diseases of tropical Africa concentrates on the former French colonies in the west and equatorial regions of the continent, including the Congo.

223 Onchocerciasis in Zaïre: a new approach to the problem of river blindness.
Edited by F. C. Rodger. New York, Oxford: Pergamon Press, 1977. 195p.
Onchocerciasis, or river blindness, is a disease borne by black flies (*Simulium*) which breed along fast flowing rivers and streams in the tropical zones of Africa and Latin America. Accompanied by ten pages of plates, this report of the medical research team on the 1974-75 Zaïre River Expedition is of great use to doctors, medical researchers and others working in the health sector in the Congo.

Health

224 **The AIDS pandemic in Africa.**
Dennis C. Weeks. *Current History*, (May 1992), p. 208-13.
'By the year 2000, approximately 25 million Africans' could be infected with HIV, the virus that causes AIDS. 'How can one begin to discuss the broad implications of HIV infection and AIDS for the poorest continent on earth, where average annual government health-care expenditures are about two US dollars for each man, woman and child?' Asking this question, Weeks goes on to describe AIDS in Africa and its present and potential effects on the continent. Little specific information on the Congo is included in this general article. However, such a survey is important in placing the situation in the Congo in its wider context.

Les tse-tses. (The tsetses.)
See item no. 55.

Bulletin de l'Institut de Recherches Scientifiques au Congo. (Bulletin of the Institute for Scientific Research in the Congo.)
See item no. 515.

Politics

General

225 Coups and army rule in Africa: studies in military style.
Edited by Samuel Decalo.   New Haven, Connecticut: Yale University
Press, 1990. 366p. bibliog.
One of the editor's own contributions to this well-researched work is a chapter on
'Revolutionary rhetoric and army cliques in Congo/Brazzaville', which analyses the
tribal and ideological differences within the Congolese army.

226 Ethnic soldiers: state security in a divided society.
Cynthia H. Enloe.   Harmondsworth, England: Penguin, 1980. 276p.
The politics and sociology of ethnically divided societies, such as that of the Congo, are
examined in this excellent work which deals with the military aspects of such situations.

227 The military in African politics.
W. F. Gutteridge.   London: Methuen, 1969. 166p.
Throughout the Congo's short history, military rule has been an important feature of
the country's political life. The army has been politically active and at different times
has promoted both stability and instability. From 1968 until 1992 virtually every
Congolese government was dominated by highly politicized military officers. Among
numerous ambitious soldiers, four individuals have played particularly prominent
roles: Marien Ngouabi, Joachim Yhombi-Opango, Denis Sassou-Nguesso and Louis
Sylvain Goma. Material on the Congo appears in this general study of African military
regimes. Gutteridge also wrote *Military regimes in Africa* (London: Methuen, 1975),
which updates the material in this work. A short bibliography is included in each.

228 **The military in African politics.**
Edited by J. W. Harbeson. New York: Praeger, 1987. 197p.
Supported by the School of Advanced International Studies at Johns Hopkins University in Baltimore, Maryland, this recent work on African military rule provides a good overview of a subject very relevant to the politics of the Congo.

229 **Personal rule in black Africa.**
Robert H. Jackson, Carl G. Rosberg. Berkeley, California:
University of California Press, 1982. 316p.
Jackson and Rosberg combine biography, psychology and political theory to develop a system of categorizing African leaders into four major archetypes: prince, autocrat, prophet and tyrant. The politics of the Congo features in this work as the authors describe the country's factional politics, purges, coups and the regimes of Youlou, Massamba-Débat, Ngouabi and Yhombi-Opango.

230 **Stay by your radios: documentation for a study of military government in tropical Africa.**
A. H. M. Kirk-Greene. Cambridge, England: Cambridge University Press; Leiden: Afrika-Studie-centrum, 1981. 156p.
Developing as a result of the failures of the governments which led their countries to independence, the trend toward military government in Africa in the 1960s and 1970s is the subject of this good introductory work.

231 **African armies and civil order.**
J. M. Lee. London: Chatto & Windus; New York: Praeger, 1969.
198p. bibliog.
The Congolese military can be viewed as a vigilant guardian, a stabilizing institution, a surrogate bureaucracy, a dictatorial master, a public indoctrination corps and a training ground for political adventurers. As in many other African nations in the last three decades, the Congolese armed forces have acted in all of these capacities. The roles of the military in African societies, including the Congo, are observed and analysed in this work, which contains a bibliography on pages 187 to 190.

232 **Custom and government in the lower Congo.**
Wyatt MacGaffey. Berkeley, California: University of California Press, 1970. 322p. maps. bibliog.
The government and society of the Bakongo are presented in this well-written book which includes illustrations, maps and an extensive nine-page bibliography.

233 **Afrocommunism.**
Marina Ottoway, David Ottoway. New York: Africana (Holmes & Meier), 1981. 237p.
Marxist-Leninism was the official ideology of the Congo for a number of years. The Ottoways examine the nature of communism, communist states and communist movements in Africa in the two decades following the break-up of the great colonial empires. Though now dated, this book provides a good general view of African revolutionaries and reactions to them. However, like so many works on African

politics, the role of ideology has been overestimated and that of ethnicity and religion undervalued.

234 **Les coups d'état militaires en Afrique noire.** (Military coup d'Etats in black Africa.)
Jean-Pierre Pabanel.   Paris: Éditions L'Harmattan, 1984. 188p.
bibliog.

This French-language book provides a good introduction to, and analysis of, military coup d'etats Sub-Saharan Africa. Military politics and the various coups experienced by the Congo feature in this work.

235 **Paths in the rainforests.**
Jan Vansina.   Madison, Wisconsin: University of Wisconsin Press, 1990. 428p. maps. bibliog.

Subtitled 'toward a history of political tradition in equatorial Africa', this work examines the political traditions of the Bantu-speaking tribes of the Congo, Zaïre and other central African nations. An excellent bibliography (p. 375-409), maps and other illustrations are included.

Colonial administration

236 **French colonialism 1871-1914: myths and realities.**
Henri Brunschwig.   London: Pall Mall, 1966. 228p.

First published in French in 1960, this authoritative overview remains one of the most important works on the establishment of the French colonial empire.

237 **Rulers of empire: the French Colonial Service in Africa.**
William B. Cohen.   Stanford, California: Hoover Institution Press, 1971. 279p. bibliog.

This book is the best English-language study of French colonial administration. Illustrations and a good bibliography (p. 249-72) are included.

238 **La nouvelle politique indigène pour l'Afrique Equatoriale Française.**
(The new indigenous politics of French Equatorial Africa.)
Félix Eboué.   Brazzaville: Afrique Française Libre, 1941; Paris: Office Français d'Education, 1944. 61p.

In this influential and historically important treatise, Eboué, the first black French colonial governor, describes the need for increased political participation by Africans in French Equatorial Africa and outlines his reform plans for after the Second World War. Although he died before the war's end, many of his suggestions were taken to heart by De Gaulle and other French leaders.

239 **Colonialism in Africa 1870-1960.**
Edited by Lewis H. Gann, Peter Duignan. Cambridge, England:
Cambridge University Press, 1970. 5 vols. bibliog.

This authoritative reference work on European imperialism in Africa includes many sections on or directly related to the Congo. In Volume One, 'French Exploration and Conquest in Tropical Africa from 1865 to 1898' by Henri Brunschwig (p. 132-64); and 'French Colonization in Africa to 1920' by Catherine Coquery-Vidrovitch (p. 165-98.) are useful in a study of the colonial era Congo. In Volume Two the following chapters are useful: 'French Colonial Policy in Black Africa' by Robert Delavignette and 'France in Black Africa and Madagascar between 1920 and 1945' by Hubert J. Deschamps. Volume 5 is a highly detailed bibliography.

240 **The rulers of German Africa 1884-1914.**
Lewis H. Gann, Peter Duignan. Stanford, California: Stanford
University Press, 1977. 286p. bibliog.

A good background study of German colonialism before the First World War, this book includes information and insights on the attitudes, structures, interests and individuals prominent in German Africa. Of particular interest to those studying the Congo are those officials connected with German attempts to establish a presence on the Sangha and Congo rivers.

241 **France and Britain in Africa: imperial rivalry and colonial rule.**
Edited by P. Gifford, W. R. Louis. New Haven, Connecticut: Yale
University Press, 1971. 989p. bibliog.

The competition between the French and British over the domination of Africa, and the role of French Equatorial Africa in the struggle are documented in this lengthy book, which also features a good bibliographical essay by David Gardinier (p. 903-950).

242 **Transfers of power in Africa.**
Edited by P. Gifford, W. R. Louis. New Haven, Connecticut: Yale
University Press, 1982. 654p. bibliog.

The important work discusses the decolonization process in Africa from 1940 to 1960. It includes Elikia M'Bokolo's 'French Colonial Policy in Equatorial Africa in the 1940s and 1950s' and ends with David E. Gardinier's bibliographical and historiographical essay on decolonization.

243 **One hundred million Frenchmen: the assimilation theory in French colonial policy.**
Martin D. Lewis. *Comparative Studies in Society and History* (The Hague), vol. 4, no. 2 (Jan. 1962), p. 129-53.

One of the leading goals of colonialism in general, and French colonialism in particular, was the assimilation of colonial subjects into the culture of the colonialist power. The subject of this article is this ambition, which was seldom realized but nevertheless had a profound effect on French policy in the colonies and is evident in French administrative, commercial and religious activities in the Congo.

244 **Les assemblées legislatives dans les etats de l'ancienne Afrique Equatoriale Française.** (Legislative assemblies in the states of old French Equatorial Africa.)
Julien Matongo. Unpublished PhD thesis. University of Paris, 1968. 436p.

Matongo's thesis describes the various legislative bodies set up by the French in equatorial Africa and the region's rapid transformation from a subject area of the French Empire to an independent constitutional republic driven by electoral politics. The early failures of electoral and parliamentary processes are rooted in the rapidity and inexperience with which the system moved, and the particularistic politics of many of the leaders of the emerging nations of the Congo, Gabon, Chad and the Central African Republic.

245 **The history of French colonial policy 1870-1925.**
Stephen H. Roberts. London: King, 1929. 2 vols.

This is one of the most comprehensive introductions to French colonialism available in English.

246 **La politique Africaines du General de Gaulle 1958-1969.** (The African politics of General de Gaulle 1958-1969.)
Pedone, France: Centre d'Etude d'Afrique Noire, Institut d'Etude Politique de Bordeaux, 1980. 421p.

This work concentrates on the gaining of independence for France's African colonies and Paris' continuing influence in and support for its former possessions. Charles de Gaulle, who played a major role in implementing these policies, is given particular consideration.

Histoire des colonies Françaises et de l'expansion Française dans le monde. (A history of French colonies and French expansion in the world.)
See item no. 77.

France and the Africans, 1944-1960.
See item no. 83.

French colonialism in tropical Africa 1900-1945.
See item no. 88.

De Brazza à Gentil: la politique Française en Haute-Sangha à la fin du XIXe siècle. (De Brazza to Gentil: French politics in Upper Sangha to the end of the 19th century.)
See item no. 102.

Chroniques d'Outre-Mer. (Overseas chronicles.)
See item no. 518.

A historical dictionary of the People's Republic of the Congo.
See item no. 526.

Politics and government in former French West and Equatorial Africa: a critical bibliography.
See item no. 527.

Bibliographie de l'Afrique Equatoriale Française. (A bibliography of French Equatorial Africa.)
See item no. 528.

Guide bibliographique sommaire d'histoire militaire et coloniale Françaises. (A concise bibliographic guide to French military and colonial history.)
See item no. 530.

Official publications of French Equatorial Africa, French Cameroons and Togo, 1946-1958.
See item no. 534.

Post-colonial politics

247 **Benin, the Congo, Burkina Faso: economics, politics and society.**
Christopher Allen, (et al.). New York, London: Printer, 1988. 300p. bibliog.

Originally published by L. Rienner (Boulder, Colorado: 1985), this general overview of the government, politics, economy and social conditions of three of Francophone Africa's lesser known countries was part of the publisher's Marxist Regimes Series. Three common threads which run throughout this excellent work are these countries' French colonial heritage, Marxist orientations and increasing dependence on foreign creditors. The material on the Congo is written by Michael S. Radu and Keith Somerville.

248 **The development of political parties in French Equatorial Africa.**
John A. Ballard. Unpublished PhD thesis. Fletcher School of Tufts University. Medford, Massachusetts, 1963. 675p. bibliog.

Ethnicity has proved to be the principal motivating force behind the rise of political parties in the Congo and the other states of former French Equatorial Africa. This excellent thesis, which examines the formation of these organizations, includes illustrations and a good bibliography (p. 650-75).

249 **Four equatorial states.**
John A. Ballard. In: *National Unity and Regionalism in Eight African States*. Edited by Gwendolen M. Carter. Ithaca, New York: Cornell University Press, 1966. p. 231-329.

Ballard's chapter on the nations formed from French Equatorial Africa includes material on the background to Congolese independence, internal political forces, tribalism and the policies of the Youlou regime. This book was widely distributed and very influential in its time.

250 **New youth class in Congo (Brazzaville).**
Pierre Bonnafe. *US Joint Publications Research Service Translations on Africa* (Washington, DC), no. 676 (1968), p. 66-78.
The background to the establishment of the Jeunesse du Mouvement National de la Révolution is discussed in this translation of an article which appeared in *Revue* (Brussels, Institut de Sociologie, no. 2-3, 1967, p. 321-35).

251 **Le Congo, formation sociale et mode developpement economique.** (The Congo, social formation and economic development.)
Hugues Bertrand.   Paris: Maspero, 1975. 320p.
This is a good general work on the politics of social and economic development in the Congo.

252 **Ideological rhetoric and scientific socialism in Benin and Congo-Brazzaville.**
Sameul Decalo.   In: *Socialism is Sub-Saharan Africa: a new assessment*. Edited by Carl G. Roseberg, Thomas M. Callaghy.
Berkeley, California: University of California Press, 1979. p. 231-64.
Decalo examines the degree to which the espousal of leftist socialism in the Congo has been a façade.

253 **The politics of Congo-Brazzaville.**
René Gauze.   Stanford, California: Hoover Institution Press, 1973. 283p. bibliog.
One of the few full length books on Congolese politics in English, Gauze's work was translated, edited and supplemented by Virginia Thompson and Richard Adloff. This book includes some illustrations.

254 **Political integration in French-speaking Africa.**
Abdul Aziz Jalloh.   Berkeley, California: Institute of International Studies of the University of California, 1973. 208p. bibliog.
The government, politics and political integration of both former French Equatorial Africa and former French West Africa are surveyed in this study of the various French-dominated organizations in the region.

255 **Decrees resolving and setting up various army units and listing cadres of active ground forces in Congo (Brazzaville).**
JPRS.   *US Joint Publications Research Service Translations on Africa* (Washington, DC), no. 406 (1966), p. 20-35.
This translation of a series of decrees published in the *Journal Officiel de la République du Congo* (Brazzaville, 1 March 1966, p. 197-202) provides a look at one of the many reorganizations of the Congolese army.

256 **'Scientific socialism' in the Congo-Brazzaville.**
JPRS. *US Joint Publications Research Service Translations on Africa*
(Washington, DC), no. 718 (1968), p. 38-46.

Marxism in the Congo is the subject of this translation of articles in various January
and February 1968 issues of *La Tribune Africaine* (Kinshasa). This piece fails,
however, to recognize the degree to which ideology is a façade for tribalism.

257 **Clan loyalties and socialist doctrine in the People's Republic of the
Congo.**
J. M. Lee. *The World Today*, vol. 27, no. 1 (Jan. 1971), p. 40-6.

Lee offers an excellent analysis of the uncertainties generated by the Congo's system of
clan patronage and factional politics in comparison to the official leftist doctrines of the
country's governments in the late 1960s.

258 **Balance sheet of the two years of the administration of the Congolese
revolutionary regime.**
Pascal Lissouba. *US Joint Publications Research Service Translations
on Africa* (Washington, DC), no. 256 (1965), p. 21-33.

Lissouba's views on Congolese politics have become increasingly important, since as
President he is leading the Congo during the nation's efforts to establish multi-party
politics, a free market economy and a pro-Western foreign policy in the 1990s. In this
translated article he evaluates the Congolese revolutionary regime which toppled the
country's first president.

259 **Conscience du développement et démocratie.** (Developmental
conscience and democracy.)
Pascal Lissouba. Dakar: Nouvelles Éditions Africaines, 1975. 75p.

Prefaced by Samir Amin, this book is a series of reflections by the former Prime
Minister, now President Lissouba, on his country's colonial influences, socialism, and
economic and social policies at a time when he was out of favour with the
revolutionary elite in Brazzaville.

260 **Congo-Brazzaville president criticizes MNR party extremists.**
Alphonse Massamba-Débat. *US Joint Publications Research Service
Translations on Africa* (Washington, DC), no. 618 (1967), p. 27-42.

Originally reported in the *Bulletin Quotiden de l'ACI* (Brazzaville), (4 July 1967), p. 1-
16 , Massamba-Débat's speech criticized extremist radicals within his Mouvement
National de la Révolution, who opposed his 'technocratic' approach to socialism.

261 **President Massamba-Débat stresses importance of work for Congo
(Brazzaville) revolution.**
Alphonse Massamba-Débat. *US Joint Publications Research Service
Translations on Africa* (Washington, DC), no. 628 (1967), p. 17-24.

This speech, presented to the annual congress of the Jeunesse du Mouvement National
de la Révolution and translated from *Dipanda* (Brazzaville, 23 July 1967, p. 1 & 5), is
a good example of Massamba-Débat's style and pedantic approach to government.

262   **Massamba-Débat's concept of scientific socialism discussed.**
Albert G. N'Gbanzo. *US Joint Publications Research Service Translations on Africa* (Washington, DC), no. 707 (1968), p.74-81.
Massamba-Débat's political philosophy is described in this translation of an article series from *La Tribune Africaine* (Kinshasa, 27 Jan.-1 Feb. 1968).

263   **Vers la construction d'une société socialiste en Afrique.** (Towards the construction of a socialist society in Africa.)
Marien Ngouabi. Paris: Présence Africaine, 1975. 727p.
Prior to his assassination, Congolese President Ngouabi described his style of socialism and his hopes for the Congo's future in this lengthy book which includes twenty-two pages of photographs. In addition to those works translated below, the speeches and writings of Ngouabi can also be found in two books which are more difficult to acquire: *Rectifions Notre Style de Travail* (Brazzaville: Government of the Congo, 1974) and *Les Paroles du Président Marien Ngouabi* (Brazzaville: Government of the Congo, 1978).

264   **Ngouabi comments on foreign relations, domestic policies.**
Marien Ngouabi. *US Joint Publications Research Service Translations on Africa* (Washington, DC), no. 1227 (1972), p. 2-13.
These translated excerpts of an interview with President Ngouabi in the *Bulletin Quotidien de l'ACI* (Brazzaville), (25 Sept. 1972, p. 6-19.) provide some perspectives on his policies.

265   **PCT head urges continued revolutionary posture.**
Marien Ngouabi. *US Joint Publications Research Service Translations on Africa* (Washington, DC), no. 894 (1970), p. 65-79.
As leader of the Congo's sole legal political party, the Parti Congolais du Travail, Ngouabi maintained the country's Marxist stance in this speech, translated from the *Bulletin Quotidien de l'ACI* (Brazzaville), (2 April 1970, p. 1-14.)

266   **L'administration Congolaise.** (Congolese administration.)
Claude C. Pereira. Paris: Berger-Levrault, 1979. 81p. bibliog.
This short book provides a good summary of Congolese administrative law.

267   **Congolese revolutionary progress analyzed.**
Luigi Pestalozza. *US Joint Publications Research Service Translations on Africa* (Washington, DC), no. 827 (1969), p. 3-13.
The Marxist-inspired revolution in the Congo is discussed in this translation of an article in *Rinascita* (Rome), (28 Sept. 1969), p. 23-4.

268   **Progress made by revolution analyzed.**
Renato Sesana. *US Joint Publications Research Service Translations on Africa* (Washington, DC), no. 1093 (1971), p. 54-62.
These translated excerpts from an article in *Nigrizia* (Verona), (Nov. 1971), p. 4-9, examine the Congo's revolutionary regime eight years after the ousting of Youlou.

269 **The Congo (Brazzaville) and neo-colonialism.**
  H. de Schrijver. *US Joint Publications Research Service Translations on Africa* (Washington, DC), no. 259 (1965), p. 10-23.
The Congo's continued reliance on French trade, aid, technical personnel and investment is criticized in this translation of a series of four articles in *Volkstimme* (Vienna), published during August and September 1965.

270 **The emerging states of French Equatorial Africa.**
  Virginia Thompson, Richard Adloff. Stanford, California: Stanford University Press; Oxford: Oxford University Press, 1960. 595p. bibliog.
Complete with illustrations and maps, this is the most widely read and one of the best books in English on the politics and political history of French Equatorial Africa from the outbreak of the Second World War until the granting of independence to the former French African colonies. Today much of the information is of historical use only.

271 **Patrimonialism and changes in the Congo.**
  Jean Claude Willaure. Stanford, California: Stanford University Press, 1972. 223p. bibliog.
Investigating beyond the superficial politics of ideology, long before it was fashionable to do so, Millaure examines the changing patron-client relationships of the Congo basin.

272 **J'accuse la Chine.** (I accuse China.)
  Fulbert Youlou. Paris: La Table Ronde, 1966. 253p.
The degree to which the spread of Chinese communist influence had become an obsession with Youlou, the first president of the Congo, is evident in this rambling work which seems to blame Peking for most of Africa's difficulties.

273 **Comment sauver l'Afrique.** (How to save Africa.)
  Fulbert Youlou. Troyes, France: Paton, 1968. 23p.
The ousted first president of the Congo, Fulbert Youlou expressed his concerns with the spread of communist influence in Africa generally, and particularly in the Congo, in this short monograph.

Congo: profile.
See item no. 1.

Area handbook for the People's Republic of the Congo (Congo Brazzaville).
See item no. 3.

Histoire et sociologie politiques du Congo. (A history and political sociology of the Congo.)
See item no. 116.

Bulletin de l'Afrique noire. (Bulletin of black Africa.)
See item no. 302.

Europe France Outre-mer. (Europe France overseas.)
See item no. 308.

Congo, Gabon, Equatorial Guinea: country report, analyses of economic and political trends.
See item no. 311.

Congo: country profile, annual survey of political and economic background.
See item no. 312.

Quarterly review of Gabon, Congo, Cameroon, the Central African Republic, Chad and Equatorial Guinea.
See item no. 313.

Marchés Tropicaux. (Tropical markets.)
See item no. 316.

Le Moniteur Africain. (The African monitor.)
See item no. 317.

Africa Confidential.
See item no. 477.

Africa Report.
See item no. 478.

AfricAsia.
See item no. 479.

Afrique nouvelle. (New Africa.)
See item no. 480.

Bulletin Quotidien de l'ACI. (Daily bulletin of the ACI.)
See item no. 482.

Dipanda. (Independence.)
See item no. 484.

Etumba. (Star.)
See item no. 485.

Jeune Afrique. (Young Africa.)
See item no. 489.

Journal Officiel de la Republique du Congo. (Official Journal of the Republic of the Congo.)
See item no. 490.

Le Monde. (The world.)
See item no. 491.

Le Monde diplomatique. (The diplomatic world.)
See item no. 492.

Politics. Post-colonial politics

La Semaine. (The Week.)
See item no. 495.

West Africa.
See item no. 496.

Africa research bulletin.
See item no. 514.

The Congo.
See item no. 521.

Keesing's contemporary archives.
See item no. 522.

Encyclopedia of the Third World.
See item no. 523.

Africa contemporary record.
See item no. 524.

Le Mois en Afrique. (The month in Africa.)
See item no. 525.

A historical dictionary of the People's Republic of the Congo.
See item no. 526.

Constitution and Legal System

274 Amnesty International reports.
Amnesty International. London: Amnesty International, annual.
Amnesty International provides in its annual reports a review of human rights violations worldwide. The Congo has been covered by articles in issues throughout the 1970s and 1980s. The appendices related to the international protection of human rights are useful references.

275 Law and judicial systems of nations.
Anonymous. Washington, DC: World Peace through Law Center, 1965.
The judicial system of the Congo, as it stood under the Massamba-Débat regime, is described on pages 35-39 of this directory of lawyers, judiciaries and law schools.

276 The legal status of communes in country discussed.
François Bigemi. *US Joint Publications Research Service Translations on Africa* (Washington, DC), no. 733. (1968), p. 86-94.
The legal role of local administrative units is described in this translation of Bigemi's article in *Revue Juridique et Politique* (April/June 1968, p. 363-370).

277 Congo (Brazzaville).
In: *Constitutions of the Countries of the World*. Edited by A. P. Blaustein, G. H. Flanz. New York: Oceana, 1971- . 3 vols. annual.
The Congo (Brazzaville) section of this continually updated loose-leaf reference work provided the text of the 1979 Rwandan Constitution in its 1981 edition, with amendments in more recent issues. Back issues provide the text for the 1963, 1970 and 1973 Congolese constitutions.

Constitution and Legal System

278 **Constitution of Congo-Brazzaville communist inspired.**
Pierre Decheix. *US Joint Publications Research Service Translations
on Africa* (Washington, DC), no. 939 (1970), p. 55-61.
The Marxist orientation of the 3 January 1970 Congolese constitution is described in
this translation of an article from *Revue Juridique et Politique* (Jan.-March 1970,
p. 111-6).

279 **Law number 29-64 of 9 September 1964 establishing people's courts.**
JPRS. *US Joint Publications Research Service Translations on Africa*
(Washington, DC), no. 146 (1964), p. 39-52.
This repressive nature of the Massamba-Débat regime is amply illustrated in this
translation of the text of this important law as it appeared in *Journal Officiel de la
République du Congo* (15 Sept. 1964, p. 753-6).

280 **MNR Paris section report at 8th AEC congress asks revision of Congo
(Brazzaville) constitution.**
JPRS. *US Joint Publications Research Service Translations on Africa*
(Washington, DC), no. 378 (1966), p. 17-25.
Dissatisfied with the 1963 constitution, activists in the Mouvement National de la
Revolution, the only official Congolese political party under the Massamba-Débat
regime, called for revision of the document on more leftist lines at the eighth annual
congress of the Association des Étudiants Congolais. These moves were originally
reported in *La Voix de la Révolution* (26 March 1966, p. 3 & 5).

281 **New Congo (Brazzaville) constitution text given.**
JPRS. *US Joint Publications Research Service Translations on Africa*
(Washington, DC), no. 857 (1970), p. 35-42.
This is a translation of the text of the 1970 Congolese constitution from the *Bulletin
Quotidien de l'ACI* (5 Jan. 1970, p. 1-8).

282 **Customary land law in Africa.**
Frank M. Mifsud. Rome: Food and Agriculture Organization, 1967.
96p.
Issues of land tenure, inheritance and succession are examined in this short reference
work which is applicable to the Congo. A short bibliography is included.

283 **Les politiques penales en Afrique noire Francophone: le cas du Gabon.**
(Penal politics in French-speaking black Africa: the case of Gabon.)
Frederique Pie. Bordeaux, France: Institut d'Etudes Politiques de
Universite de Bordeaux I, 1989. 195p. bibliog.
Although concentrating on Gabon, this recent work examines and compares criminal
law in the Congo and other Francophone central African countries, as well as some
former French colonies in west Africa.

284   **Revue juridique et politique: independence et cooperation.** (Legal and
      political review: independence and co-operation.)
      Paris: Ediafric, 1964- . quarterly.

First known as the *Revue Juridique et Politique de l'Union Française*, then as the *Revue
Juridique et Politique d'Outre-Mer* and finally by the present title, this French-language
law and politics journal has published numerous articles on the Congo, including J.
Ganga-Zandzou's 'Responsabilité des chefs de groupements coutumiers au Congo'
(Responsibilities of customary chiefs in the Congo. Oct.-Dec. 1973); and also the
French language originals of items 276 and 278.

Bulletin Quotidien de l'ACI. (Daily bulletin of the ACI.)
See item no. 482.

Encyclopedia of the Third World.
See item no. 523.

Foreign Relations

Colonial

285 **African boundaries: a legal and diplomatic encyclopedia.**
Ian Brownlie. London: Hurst, 1979. 1355p.

This huge work, which contains numerous treaty texts, is by far the most important reference work on national borders in Africa. Of interest to those studying the Congo are the sections on the Congo, Zaïre and Gabon.

Les Relations economiques exterieures des pays d'Afrique noire de l'Union Française. (The foreign economic relations of the black African countries of the French Union.)
See item no. 332.

Post-colonial

286 **A certain mystery: how can France do everything that it does in Africa – and get away with it?**
Tamar Golan. *African Affairs*, vol. 80 (1981), p. 3-12.

Golan examines the continuing close relationships between France and her former African possessions, including the Congo, as an explanation for the high level of French influence in black Africa.

287 **Communist powers and sub-Saharan Africa.**
  Edited by Thomas H. Henriksen.   Stanford, California: Hoover
  Institution Press, 1981. 137p. bibliog.

This general overview of relations between the Soviet Bloc and black Africa before *glasnost* includes some material on the Congo.

288 **China and Africa 1949 – 1970.**
  Bruce D. Larkin.   Berkeley, California: University of California Press,
  1971. 260p. bibliog.

Sino-African relations remains a largely unstudied topic. This book provides valuable background information necessary for understanding this interesting relationship. Chapters include an analysis of the history of the Chinese presence in Africa; economic relations; ideological issues; setbacks; the Chinese revolutionary model; African states and liberation movements; and prospects and probabilities. As the Congo was one of the first black African nations to recognize the People's Republic of China, it is not surprising that much space is devoted to Sino-Congolese relations, including material on the establishment of diplomatic relations, liberation movements based in the Congo, Chinese influence and aid, Chinese visitors to the Congo and Chinese impressions of the country. Throughout the second half of the 1960s and the early 1970s, Chinese aid and influence in the Congo was greater than any other major power except France in terms of volume and variety. However, after Angolan independence, the Chinese were eclipsed by the Soviets and Cubans.

289 **France in black Africa.**
  Francis T. McNamara.   Washington, DC: National Defense
  University, 1989. 289p.

Sponsored by the United States government, McNamara's study provides a good general overview of French colonial history, diplomacy and influences in tropical Africa. Illustrations and bibliographical references are included.

290 **Congo-Zaïre boundary.**
  Office of the Geographer.   Washington, DC: US Department of State,
  1972. 7p.

This short report, meant to describe the exact location of the Congo's eastern and southern border on an accompanying map, is number 127 in the US State Department's International Boundary Studies.

291 **China's policy in Africa, 1958-1971.**
  Alaba Ogunsanwo.   Cambridge, England: Cambridge University
  Press, 1974. 310p. bibliog.

An African view of Chinese influence in Africa in the 1960s is provided in this well-written study.

292 **United States treaties and other international acts.**
US Department of State.   Washington, DC: US Department of State.
irregular.

The texts of all American treaties are published in this series of publically available
official documents. Those dealing with the Congo include two interesting agreements
concluded under US President John F. Kennedy: a pact in which the Congolese
government recognized the continued application of treaties concerning the Congo
which had been signed prior to Congolese independence by the USA and France (no.
5161 – signed in Brazzaville on 12 May & 5 August 1961) and investment guaranties
between the USA and the Congo (no. 5183 – signed in Brazzaville on 26 July & 1
September 1962.) More recent treaties of interest include an agricultural commodities
agreement (no. 91-335-P – signed in Brazzaville on 16 August 1982) and accords
concerning reciprocal encouragement and protection of investment (no. 102-1 – signed
in Washington, DC on 12 February 1990).

Congo: profile.
See item no. 1.

**A survey of political, economic and sociological development in the Congo
(Brazzaville).**
See item no. 2.

Background notes on the Congo.
See item no. 4.

**Le problème de regroupement en Afrique equatoriale: du régime colonial à
l'Union Douanière et Economique de l'Afrique Centrale.** (The problem of
regrouping in equatorial Africa: from the colonial regime to the Central
African Customs and Economic Union.)
See item no. 307.

Europe France Outre-mer. (Europe France overseas.)
See item no. 308.

Marchés Tropicaux. (Tropical markets.)
See item no. 316.

**Trade and development aspects of the Central African Customs and Economic
Union (UDEAC).**
See item no. 318.

French development assistance: a study in policy and administration.
See item no. 321.

**Do the benefits of fixed exchange rates outweigh their costs?: the Franc zone in
Africa.**
See item no. 327.

**The banking system of Gabon and the Central Bank of Equatorial Africa and
Cameroon.**
See item no. 328.

IMF staff papers.
See item no. 329.

Les Relations economiques exterieures des pays d'Afrique noire de l'Union Française. (The foreign economic relations of the black African countries of the French Union.)
See item no. 332.

Market brief for the US agricultural development/agribusiness trade mission to the Congo, Cameroon and Nigeria, June 29-July 18 1985.
See item no. 333.

Dipanda. (Independence.)
See item no. 484.

Le Mois en Afrique. (The month in Africa.)
See item no. 525.

The Economy and Economic Development

General

293 **Histoire économique du Congo 1880-1968.** (An economic history of the Congo 1880-1968.)
S. Amin, C. Coquery-Vidrovitch. Paris: Anthropos; Dakar: IFAN, 1969. 204p. maps. bibliog.

This excellent French-language study of the economy of the Congo extends from the time of the establishment of French Equatorial Africa to the founding of the Union Douaniere et Economique d'Afrique Centrale.

Area handbook for the People's Republic of the Congo (Congo Brazzaville).
See item no. 3.

Pre-colonial and colonial

294 **La mise en valeur de l'Afrique Equatoriale Française.** (Investment in French Equatorial Africa.)
Anonymous. Casablanca, Morocco: Éditions Fontana-Maroc, 1956. 358p. maps.

A study of the post-Second World War economic and social conditions in the Congo and the other component parts of French Equatorial Africa is provided in this illustrated work.

295 **La crise economique au Congo Belge et en Afrique Equatorial Française.**
(The economic crisis in the Belgian Congo and French Equatorial
Africa.)
Comite Franco-Belge d'Etudes Coloniales.   Paris: Comité Franco-
Belge d'Etudes Coloniales, 1930. 50p.

An official European view of the economic conditions in present-day Zaïre, Gabon,
Chad, the Central African Republic and the Congo during the Great Depression.

296 **The concession policy in the French Congo and the British reaction 1897-
1906.**
S. J. S. Cookey.   *Journal of African History*, vol. 7, no. 2 (July 1966),
p. 263-78.

A scandal in its time, the much criticized concessionary system which allowed French
interests to exploit the Congo after de Brazza had left the colonial administration is the
subject of this excellent brief article, which also looks at the British reactions which led
to the system's exposure and reform.

297 **Le Congo au temps des grandes compagnies concessionnaires 1898-1930.**
(The Congo in the time of the great concessionary companies 1898-
1930.)
Catherine Coquery-Vidrovitch.   Paris: Mouton, 1972. 598p.

Focusing on the rise and fall of concessionary companies, this book is the definitive
study of the pre-Second World War economy of French Equatorial Africa.

298 **The external trade of the Loango coast 1576-1870.**
Phyllis M. Martin.   Oxford: Clarendon, 1972. 193p.

An excellent study of the effects of changing commercial relations, including the slave
trade, on the Vili Kingdom of Loango.

299 **La Compagnie de l'Ogooué: son influence géographique au Gabon et au
Congo.** (The Ogooue company: its geographical influence on Gabon
and the Congo.)
Marie-Louise Villien-Rossi.   Paris: Honoré Champion, 1978. 700p.

The commercial and transport connections forged by the French between Gabon and
the Congo are throughly presented in this lengthy French-language work.

**British views of the importance of French Africa to the Allied war effort 1940-
1944.**
See item no. 68.

African history.
See item no. 73.

The Atlantic slave trade: a census.
See item no. 74.

Black cargoes: a history of the Atlantic slave trade 1518-1865.
See item no. 81.

Cahiers d'études Africaines. (African studies notes.)
See item no. 516.

Cahiers d'outre-mer. (Overseas notes.)
See item no. 517.

Encyclopédie coloniale et maritime, volume V. (Colonial and maritime encyclopedia, volume V.)
See item no. 519.

Post-colonial

300 **African business.**
London: IC, 1966-. monthly.
This British-based magazine, formerly *African Development*, regularly reports Congolese economic and business news.

301 **Bingo.**
Dakar, Paris: Feb. 1953-. monthly.
An optimistic article in the 22 August 1968 issue of this magazine, sub-titled 'A monthly of the black world', examines the economic wealth and possible development of the Congo. Developments are also surveyed in articles throughout September 1969.

302 **Bulletin de l'Afrique noire.** (Bulletin of black Africa.)
Paris: Ediafric, 1957-. weekly.
This review of economic affairs in black Africa has featured numerous articles on the Congo, including 'Perspective Africaine – Synthèses Politiques et Économiques' (African perspective – political and economic syntheses), which was a supplement to *Bulletin de l'Afrique Noire* (Paris) vol. 10, (29 June 1966) on the economic and political conditions prevailing in the Congo in the mid-1960s. Foreign trade statistics are given in vol. 12, (25 Sept. 1968). A look at the Congolese budget is provided in vol. 13, 11 (June 1969). A good brief overview of the Congolese economy is presented in no. 628 (13 January 1971, p. 12684-12701.) Also the *Bulletin de l'Afrique Noire* has published articles reporting on African mine production (14 June 1967); the Trans-Equatorial Communications Agency [ATEC] (29 Nov. 1967); economic development policies and plans (8 Nov. 1967, 27 Nov. 1968); timber production (13 Dec. 1967); the benefits of a European Development Fund-financed road (13 March 1968); the country's economic situation (20 March 1968); EEC aid (12 June 1968); development plans for the Kouilou region (26 June 1968); the Congolese road network (10 July 1968); trans-equatorial transport projects (13 Nov. 1968); French aid personnel in Africa (28 Dec. 1968); finance (5 June 1968, 23 April 1969); monetary policies (31 Jan. 1968, 23 April 1969) and the Congo-Ócean railway (3 Sept. 1969).

303 **Bulletin Mensuel de la Chamber de Commerce de Brazzaville.** (Monthly bulletin of the Brazzaville Chamber of Commerce.)
Brazzaville: Brazzaville Chamber of Commerce, monthly.

Since the early 1960s, this monthly publication has provided a fairly regular source of business and economic news, statistics and other information on the Congo in French.

304 **Business America.**
Washington, DC: US Department of Commerce, 1978-. biweekly.

Eager to benefit from the Congo's more open economic policies since the late 1980s, this American government periodical for business has featured short articles on the competitiveness of American products in the Congo (11 April 1988, p. 23); the outlook for business in the Congo (23 Oct. 1989, p. 24-5), the replacement of dogmatic socialism with pragmatism in the Congo (23 April 1990, p. 40) and economic conditions affecting American investments (22 Oct. 1990, p. 7.) *Business America* is the most recent title of *Commerce America*, which was previously named *Commerce Today*.

305 **Marketing in the Congo.**
Ian M. Davis.   Washington, DC: US Department of Commerce, 1988. 48p.

Sponsored by the US International Trade Administration, Davis' study of business and marketing is recent enough to be of highly significant use to businesspeople, scholars and journalists. It is one of the ITA's series of Overseas Business Reports (no. OBR 88-05).

306 **L'Oncle, le ndoki et l'entrepreneur: la petite entreprise Congolaise a Brazzaville.** (The uncle, the ndoki and the entrepreneur: Congolese small business in Brazzaville.)
Roland Devauges.   Paris: ORSTOM, 1977. 187p.

This highly interesting French-language work presents case studies of small business and entrepreneurship in Brazzaville.

307 **Le problème de regroupement en Afrique equatoriale: du régime colonial à l'Union Douanière et Economique de l'Afrique Centrale.** (The problem of regrouping in equatorial Africa: from the colonial regime to the Central African Customs and Economic Union.)
Joachim de Dreux-Brezé.   Paris: Pichon & Durand-Auzias, 1968. 214p.

The difficulties involved in co-ordinating the economies of the UDEAC nations are explained in this French-language book, written early in the process of French-encouraged integration.

308 **Europe France Outre-mer.** (Europe France overseas.)
      Paris: 1923-73. monthly.

This French economic, commercial and financial publication has produced numerous articles on the Congo. The aftermath of the 1963 ousting of Fulbert Youlou is the subject of a series of articles which appeared in November 1964. The most important of these are 'Congo-Brazzaville; 15 mois de révolution' (Congo-Brazzaville 15 months of revolution); J. C. Hubert's 'Les réalisations industrielles sont en avance sur le programmes du plan: le rôle du secteur privé' (Industrial achievement is part of the plan's programmes: the role of the private sector.) The December 1967 issue of *Europe-France Outre-Mer* contained articles on French-Congolese relations, a political, economic and sociological survey of the Congo, foreign trade, forestry, public works projects and investments. Other articles relevant to the Congo include 'Le Bois dans l'économie des principaux pays producteurs de l'Afrique noire' (Wood in the economies of the principal black African producer countries) (March 1965); P. Chauvet's 'Le Réalisme de la politique economique' (The realism of the political economy) (Dec. 1967); 'Perspectives economiques favorables à moyen terme' (Economic outlook favourable in medium term) (Dec. 1971); and shorter pieces on the European Development Fund assistance (Nov. 1964); the Francophone African cotton industry (March 1967) and African mine production and the Holle potash deposits (Sept. 1967).

309 **Europe Outre-mer.** (Europe overseas.)
      Paris: 1974-. monthly.

A continuation of *Europe France Outre-Mer* (see previous item), this French periodical has published several lengthy articles on the Congo, including 'La République Populaire du Congo' (The People's Republic of the Congo – May 1980) and 'Congo: l'economie en expansion rapide' (The Congo: the economy in rapid expansion – Dec. 1982).

310 **False start in Africa.**
      René Dumont. London: Earthscan, 1988. 304p.

Originally published in 1962 as *L'Afrique noire est mal partie*. Agronomist and development expert Dumont looks at post-colonial Africa's early failures, and proposes sustainable forms of economic development. The Congo, former French Equatorial Africa and the effects of French colonialism are described and frequently cited as examples.

311 **Congo, Gabon, Equatorial Guinea: country report, analyses of economic and political trends.**
      The Economist. London: Economist Intelligence Unit, quarterly.

This specialized publication of *The Economist* offers up-to-date economic and political information, careful analysis and numerous statistics for business, recording and predicting possible trends in the Congo, Gabon and Equatorial Guinea.

312 **Congo: country profile, annual survey of political and economic background.**
      The Economist. London: Economist Intelligence Unit, annual.

This specialized annual publication of *The Economist* offers more general economic and political information for business than that in item number 311.

313 **Quarterly review of Gabon, Congo, Cameroon, the Central African Republic, Chad and Equatorial Guinea.**
The Economist. London: Economist Intelligence Unit, quarterly.

Covering a wider geographical area than the preceding two items, this specialized publication of *The Economist* offers up-to-date economic, financial and political information for business. Accompanied by careful analysis and numerous statistics, it records and predicts possible trends in the Congo. Material on the Congo first appeared in this form in *The Economist's Quarterly Review of Former French Tropical Africa* (1960-1967), then in its *Quarterly Review of Former French Equatorial Africa, Cameroon and Madagascar* (1968-1975) and finally in its *Quarterly Economic Review of Gabon, Congo, Cameroon, the Central African Republic, Chad and Madagascar* (from 1976 until changing to the above title in 1985).

314 **Annual report.**
International Bank for Reconstruction and Development.
Washington, DC: International Bank for Reconstruction and Development, 1945-. annual.

The World Bank's annual reviews provide general economic information and statistics for all member nations. The Congo features in this data.

315 **Interim development plan of the Congo (Brazzaville).**
JPRS. *US Joint Publications Research Service Translations on Africa* (Washington, DC), no. 55 (1964), p. 45-76.

The Massamba-Débat regime quickly wrote this economic plan following the 1963 coup d'etat. This is a translation of the official plan published on 2 May 1964.

316 **Marchés Tropicaux.** (Tropical markets.)
Paris: Nov. 1945-. weekly.

Known also as *Marchés Tropicaux et Méditerranéens* (Tropical and Mediterranean markets), Marchés Tropicaux has published and continues to publish regular articles of particular interest to businessmen operating in French-speaking Africa. Past pieces on the Congo include 'Redressement sûr mais difficile du Congo' (The Congo's certain but difficult stabilization), vol. 20, (1 August 1964); 'Le Marché d'Afrique équatoriale' (The equatorial African market), vol. 21, (30 Oct. 1965); 'A la recherche d'une harmonisation des activités' (On the research into harmonization of activities), vol. 23, (4 Feb. 1967); 'Le Congo-Brazzaville poursuit sa politique dans un climat de coopération avec la France' (The Congo-Brazzaville pursues its politics in a climate of co-operation with France), vol. 23, (24 June 1967); 'M. Massamba-Débat clarifie une situation ambiguë' (Massamba-Débat clarifies the uncertain situation), vol. 24, (20 Jan. 1968); 'Remous au Congo-Brazzaville' (Currents in the Congo-Brazzaville), vol. 24, (26 Oct. 1968); 'La Conjoncture economique nécessite des actions immédiates, en prélude au prochain plan 1970-1975' (The economic situation necessitates immediate action, in prelude to the next plan 1970-1975), vol. 25, (19 April 1969); 'Le Congo-Brazzaville à l'avant-garde de la révolution' (The Congo-Brazzaville in the forefront of the revolution), vol. 26, (17 Jan. 1970); 'Le Congo-Brazzaville accentue encore davantage l'orientation socialiste de son economie' (The Congo-Brazzaville stresses the disadvantage of the socialist orientation of its economy), vol. 26, (12 Sept. 1970); 'Le Régime de la République Populaire du Congo se radicalise' (The regime of the People's Republic of the Congo radicalizes itself), vol. 27, (24 April 1971); 'La

The Economy and Economic Development. Post-colonial

Conjoncture economique au Congo' (Economic circumstances in the Congo), vol. 29, (8 June 1973); Jacques Latrémolière's 'La Fortune au Congo' (The luck of the Congo), vol. 31, (6 June 1975); 'Un Tournant difficile pour le nouveau gouvernement de la République Populaire du Congo (A difficult turn for the new government of the People's Republic of the Congo), vol. 35, (6 April 1979); and 'Brazzaville: comment maitriser une economie pétrolière' (Brazzaville: how to control a petroleum economy), vol. 37, (6 Nov. 1981); and 'Le Congo et l'equilibre' (The Congo and the balance) by F. Gaulme, vol. 39, (5 August 1983). The 2 July 1982 number of *Marchés Tropicaux* (vol. 38) was a special issue devoted to the Congo.

317 **Le Moniteur Africain.** (The African monitor.)
     Dakar: 1961-. fortnightly (1961-2), weekly (1963-75), monthly (1976-).

Formerly known as *Le Moniteur Africain du Commerce et de l'Industrie*, this periodical is an economic review of mainly Francophone Africa. As such, UDEAC trade statistics are published periodically by this monthly. Past articles may also be of interest and use to scholars and researchers on the Congo. An article published on 1 February 1968 (p. 6 & 11) comments on the difficult social climate but favourable economic prospects of the Congo in the light of the restructuring of the administration on increasingly leftist lines. However later articles claim that official economic optimism was not fully justified (30 Oct. 1969, 29 April 1971) and that the Congo's economic prospects for 1974 caused concern (17 Jan. 1974). Other pieces of interest which contain information on the Congo, are on cattle raising (14 Aug. 1965); education (6 Oct. 1965, 19 Oct. 1966); investment credits (23 March 1966); the paper industry (2 Nov. 1967); the African construction materials industry (30 Nov. 1967); petroleum, potash and natural gas deposits (8 Feb. 1968); Francophone Africa's maritime and river fleets (11 April 1968); affairs within the Franc Zone (18 April 1968); copper (16 May 1968); gold mines (20 June 1968); the African livestock industry (8 Aug. 1968); French aid (19 Oct. 1968); public works projects (12 Dec. 1968) and the Congo's economic potential (30 Oct. 1969).

318 **Trade and development aspects of the Central African Customs and Economic Union (UDEAC).**
     Wilfred A. Ndongko.   *Cultures et Développement*, vol. 8, no. 2 (1975), p. 339-56.

This short article is an excellent introduction to the UDEAC and other Franc Zone institutions prominent in the Congo.

319 **L'Observateur Africain.** (The African observer.)
     Dakar: bimonthly.

In addition to regular news of the Congo, this periodical published an important series of articles on Congolese fishing industry, forestry sector and free enterprise in the May-June 1968 issue.

320 **Colonialisme, néo-colonialism et la transition au capitalisme: exemple de la 'Comilog' au Congo-Brazzaville.** (Colonialism, neo-colonialism and the transition to capitalism: the example of 'Comilog' in the Congo-Brazzaville.)
Pierre-Philippe Rey. Paris: Maspero, 1971. 526p.

Manganese mined at Moanda, Gabon, is transported through the Congo to world markets. Ore is carried on a forty-seven mile aerial cableway to M'Binda in the Congo for rail transport to Pointe-Noire. 'Comilog' is the Compagnie Minière de l'Ogooué, the Franco-American firm which mines the Gabonese ore. This revealing work illustrates the degree to which the Marxist Congo has co-operated with western capitalists to ensure continued revenues from transport fees. However, with the building of the Trans-Gabonese Railway, this source of income has been threatened in the 1990s.

321 **French development assistance: a study in policy and administration.**
Richard Robarts. Beverly Hills, California: Sage, 1974. 82p. bibliog.

This short, but perceptive, monograph on French economic assistance is useful in the study of development in the Congo.

322 **Basic data on the economy of the Republic of the Congo (Brazzaville).**
Charles E. Rushing. Washington, DC: US Department of Commerce, 1964. 12p. map.

This analysis of Congolese economic information five years after independence is part of the US Department of Commerce's series of Overseas Business Reports (no. OBR 64-100).

323 **Economic developments in the Republic of the Congo (Brazzaville).**
E. B. Tolman. Washington, DC: US Bureau of International Programs, 1962. 11p.

The economy of the Congo around the time of independence is well described in this report, which is Economic Report no. 62-37 of the US World Trade Information Service.

324 **Foreign economic trends and their implications for the United States: Congo.**
US Department of Commerce. Washington, DC: US Department of Commerce, 1969-. various paginations.

This irregular, but periodically updated, report offers a good deal of background material on the Congolese economy, including statistics, and information useful to foreign companies and organizations seeking to do business in or with the Congolese public and private sectors. It is prepared by the staff of the US Embassy in Brazzaville. The most recent edition of this report is dated July 1992.

325 **Investment law of the Republic of the Congo (Brazzaville).**
Arnold A. Wilken. Washington, DC: US Department of Commerce, 1962. 10p.

This survey of the Congolese investment code was presented by the US Department of Commerce as one of its Overseas Business Reports (no. OBR 62-15). Although dated it is of some historical use in depicting the Congo's foreign economic relations during the period of the Youlou regime.

Congo: profile.
See item no. 1.

A survey of political, economic and sociological development in the Congo (Brazzaville).
See item no. 2.

Abortive coup and economic program discussed.
See item no. 115.

Etudes et statistiques de la BEAC. (Studies and statistics of the Bank of Central African States.)
See item no. 326.

The banking system of Gabon and the Central Bank of Equatorial Africa and Cameroon.
See item no. 328.

IMF staff papers.
See item no. 329.

Survey of African economies.
See item no. 330.

Industries et travaux d'outre-mer. (Overseas industries and public works.)
See item no. 340.

Africa Report.
See item no. 478.

Bulletin Quotidien de l'ACI. (Daily bulletin of the ACI.)
See item no. 482.

Dipanda. (Independence.)
See item no. 484.

Etumba. (Star.)
See item no. 485.

Jeune Afrique. (Young Africa.)
See item no. 489.

La Semaine. (The Week.)
See item no. 495.

West Africa.
See item no. 496.

Africa research bulletin.
See item no. 514.

Cahiers d'outre-mer. (Overseas notes.)
See item no. 517.

The Congo.
See item no. 521.

Encyclopedia of the Third World.
See item no. 523.

Africa contemporary record.
See item no. 524.

A historical dictionary of the People's Republic of the Congo.
See item no. 526.

Finance and Banking

326 **Etudes et statistiques de la BEAC.** (Studies and statistics of the Bank of
Central African States.)
Banque des Etats de l'Afrique Centrale.   Libreville: BEAC, 1968-.
monthly.
Issues of the BEAC's monthly are valuable for Congolese financial and economic
statistics.

327 **Do the benefits of fixed exchange rates outweigh their costs?: the Franc
zone in Africa.**
S. Devarajan, D. Rodrik.   Washington, DC: World Bank, 1991. 30p.
Prepared by the World Bank's Country Economics Department, this monograph from
the series *Policy, Research and External Affairs Working Papers* offers mathematical
models and a critical look at the advantages and disadvantages of Francophone
Africa's ties to the French franc.

328 **The banking system of Gabon and the Central Bank of Equatorial Africa
and Cameroon.**
Lorenzo Frediani.   Milan, Italy: Casse di Risparmio della Provincie
Lombarde, 1974. 343p.
This work on the central African portion of the franc zone is relevant to the Congo as
background to the country's participation in the francophone Central African Customs
and Economic Union and other regional economic arrangements based on the nations
of former French Equatorial Africa.

329 IMF staff papers.
Washington, DC: International Monetary Fund, 1950-. three per annum.

These publications have over the years provided news and many details of the Congolese economy. Important early articles include 'The CFA Franc system', vol. 10, no. 3 (Nov. 1963), p. 345-96 and A. Abdel-Rahman's 'The Revenue structure of the CFA countries', vol. 12, no. 1 (March 1965), p. 73-118.

330 Survey of African economies.
International Monetary Fund. Washington, DC: International Monetary Fund, 1968-77. 7 vols.

Detailed economic and financial information and statistics on the Congo appear in Volume 1 of this annual IMF study, which is considered an authoritative source for financial and aid purposes. Specific data includes monetary, fiscal, exchange-control and trade information and material on natural resources, development planning, production, budgets, taxation, banking and payments. The text is in English and French.

Bulletin de l'Afrique noire. (Bulletin of black Africa.)
See item no. 302.

Le problème de regroupement en Afrique equatoriale: du régime colonial à l'Union Douanière et Economique de l'Afrique Centrale. (The problem of regrouping in equatorial Africa: from the colonial regime to the Central African Customs and Economic Union.)
See item no. 307.

Congo, Gabon, Equatorial Guinea: country report, analyses of economic and political trends.
See item no. 311.

Congo: country profile, annual survey of political and economic background.
See item no. 312.

Quarterly review of Gabon, Congo, Cameroon, the Central African Republic, Chad and Equatorial Guinea.
See item no. 313.

Annual report.
See item no. 314.

Marchés Tropicaux. (Tropical markets.)
See item no. 316.

Le Moniteur Africain. (The African monitor.)
See item no. 317.

Bulletin Quotidien de l'ACI. (Daily bulletin of the ACI.)
See item no. 482.

Jeune Afrique. (Young Africa.)
See item no. 489.

Finance and Banking

La Semaine. (The Week.)
See item no. 495.

Africa research bulletin.
See item no. 514.

The Congo.
See item no. 521.

Encyclopedia of the Third World.
See item no. 523.

Trade

331 Yankee traders, old coasters and African middlemen.
G. E. Brooks, Jr. Boston, Massachusetts: Boston University Press,
1970. 370p. maps. bibliog.

Described as 'a history of American legitimate trade with west Africa in the nineteenth
century', this book, which deals mainly with American trade in west Africa, provides
both the background to, and numerous details of, 19th century commerce on the
Atlantic seaboard of Africa. Illustrations are included.

**332 Les relations economiques exterieures des pays d'Afrique noire de
l'Union Française.** (The foreign economic relations of the black African
countries of the French Union.)
Jean Jacques Poquin. Paris: Colin, 1957. 297p.

Prefaced by Felix Houphouet-Boigny, this is the best study of the trading relations and
economy of French colonial Africa in the second quarter of the twentieth century. A
few illustrations and a short bibliography are provided.

**333 Market brief for the US agricultural development/agribusiness trade
mission to the Congo, Cameroon and Nigeria, June 29-July 18 1985.**
US Department of Commerce. Washington, DC: US Department of
Commerce, 1985. 28p.

Sponsored by the US Commerce Department's International Trade Administration,
this market survey of the Congolese agricultural sector describes agricultural
developments, agribusiness industries and American-Congolese relationships in these
fields.

Bulletin de l'Afrique noire. (Bulletin of black Africa.)
See item no. 302.

Trade

Business America.
See item no. 304.

Marketing in the Congo.
See item no. 305.

Le problème de regroupement en Afrique equatoriale: du régime colonial à l'Union Douanière et Economique de l'Afrique Centrale. (The problem of regrouping in equatorial Africa: from the colonial regime to the Central African Customs and Economic Union.)
See item no. 307.

Europe France Outre-mer. (Europe France overseas.)
See item no. 308.

Congo, Gabon, Equatorial Guinea: country report, analyses of economic and political trends.
See item no. 311.

Congo: country profile, annual survey of political and economic background.
See item no. 312.

Quarterly review of Gabon, Congo, Cameroon, the Central African Republic, Chad and Equatorial Guinea.
See item no. 313.

Annual report.
See item no. 314.

Marchés Tropicaux. (Tropical markets.)
See item no. 316.

Le Moniteur Africain. (The African monitor.)
See item no. 317.

Trade and development aspects of the Central African Customs and Economic Union (UDEAC).
See item no. 318.

Foreign economic trends and their implications for the United States: Congo.
See item no. 324.

Survey of African economies.
See item no. 330.

The Congo.
See item no. 521.

Encyclopedia of the Third World.
See item no. 523.

Transport and
Communications

334 Deviations speed Train Bleu.

Anonymous. *Railway Gazette International*, vol. 145, no. 2 (Feb. 1989), p. 117.

Offering information on the ninety-one km Belinga-Loubomo deviation and the prestigious Train Bleu, this article on the streamlining of the Congo-Ócean Railway is the most recent detailed news on the Congo's rail system.

335 Achievements at port of Pointe-Noire.

JPRS. *US Joint Publications Research Service Translations on Africa* (Washington, DC), no. 998 (1971), p. 8-15.

This article on the post-independence expansion of the Congo's leading port is a translation of a piece which appeared in *La Vie du Rail Outre-Mer* (Overseas railways), Paris (Jan. 1971), p. 19-23. In addition to this piece *La Vie du Rail Outre-Mer* also published two articles related to the Congo in its May 1968 issue: one on the exploitation of the Holle Potash deposits and another on programmes to handle increased rail traffic.

336 Congo-Brazzaville department of public works defends its road construction program.

H. Mounthault. *US Joint Publications Research Service Translations on Africa* (Washington, DC), no. 399 (1966), p.30-7.

A translation of Mounthault's article in *Etumba* (Brazzaville: 28 April 1966, p. 1-2 & 6), this work describes road transport policy in the Congo in its first five years of independent rule.

337 **Problems of port development in Gabon and Congo.**
Pierre Vennetier. In: *Seaports and Development in Tropical Africa.*
Edited by B. S. Hoyle, D. Hilling. London: Macmillan; New York:
Praeger, 1970. 272p. maps.

Translated from the French, Vennetier's discussion of Congolese and Gabonese port
facilities appears as Chapter 11 in this work on African seaports.

Bulletin de l'Afrique noire. (Bulletin of black Africa.)
See item no. 302.

Le Moniteur Africain. (The African monitor.)
See item no. 317.

**Colonialisme, néo-colonialism et la transition au capitalisme: exemple de la
'Comilog' au Congo-Brazzaville.** (Colonialism, neo-colonialism and the
transition to capitalism: the example of 'Comilog' in the Congo-Brazzaville.)
See item no. 320.

Bulletin Quotidien de l'ACI. (Daily bulletin of the ACI.)
See item no. 482.

Cahiers d'Outre-mer. (Overseas notes.)
See item no. 517.

The Congo.
See item no. 521.

Encyclopedia of the Third World.
See item no. 523.

Industry and Mining

**338 Causes of flour shortage debated by SIACONGO official newspaper,
SIACONGO's sales director replies to reporter's criticism.**
A. Gamboule. *US Joint Publications Research Service Translations on
Africa* (Washington, DC), no. 1269 (1973), p. 8-17.

Formed in 1970, when the Congolese government nationalized most of the country's
large agricultural and agro-industrial companies, the Société Industrielle et Agricole du
Congo (SIACONGO) collapsed in the mid-1970s when faced with overwhelming
technical, labour and marketing difficulties. An account of this aspect of the Congo's
multiple economic problems is provided by this translation of excerpts from
Gamboule's remarks in *Etumba* (27 Jan./3 Feb. 1973), p. 6, 9-10.

**339 L'industrialisation des etats de l'Union Douanière et Economique de
l'Afrique Centrale (UDEAC).** (Industrialization in the states of the
Central African Customs and Economic Union [UDEAC].)
Edited by Attilio Gaudio. *Notes et Etudes Documentaires*, no. 3830
(25 Oct. 1971), 43p.

Industry and industrial development in the equatorial African portion of the Franc
Zone is the topic of this French-language monograph.

340 Industries et travaux d'outre-mer. (Overseas industries and public
works.)
Paris: 1952-85. monthly.

This French-language review of industry, construction and public works in the
Francophone world has published the following major articles on the Congo: 'Le
Kouilou' (The Kouilou), (Sept. 1958); 'L'Activité minière au Congo est surtout axée
sur la recherche' (Mining activity in the Congo is centred chiefly on exploration),
(Sept. 1962); 'Congo (Brazzaville): le premier plan quinquennal (1964-1968) pour le
developpement économique du pays' (Congo [Brazzaville]: the first five-year plan

Industry and Mining

[1964-1968] for national economic development), (Feb. 1965); 'Les Mines au Congo-Brazzaville de 1962 à 1965' (Mines in the Congo-Brazzaville from 1962 to 1965), (Dec. 1966); 'Le Projet du chemin de fer minier de Zanaga' (The Zanaga mining railway project), (June 1967); 'Congo-Brazzaville: l'activité des travaux publics en 1967' (Congo-Brazzaville: public works activities in 1967), (Sept. 1967); 'La Mise en valeur des pays du Niari' (Investment in the Niari country), (Aug. 1968), and also articles on African railways (June 1965) and the modernization of the Congo-Ócean railway (Oct. 1968).

341 **Industrial development: prospects outlined.**
JPRS. *US Joint Publications Research Service Translations on Africa* (Washington, DC), no. 807 (1969), p.95-102.

The Congolese revolutionary regime's dreams of industrialization are described in this translation of an article in *Hommes et Organisations d'Afrique Noire* (Paris), (8 July 1969), p. 5952-56.

342 **The mineral resources of Africa.**
Nicolas de Kun. Amsterdam, New York: Elsevier, 1965. 740p. maps. bibliog.

This reference work on the mineral resources of Africa and their exploitation is accompanied by illustrations, maps and a good bibliography.

343 **The mineral economics of Africa.**
Nicolas de Kun. Amsterdam, New York: Elsevier, 1987. 345p.

Although not as detailed, this study of Africa's mineral industries and resources provides more recent information than de Kun's work in the previous item.

344 **The social and economic effects of petroleum development in non-OPEC developing countries.**
Jon B. McLin. Geneva: International Labour Office, 1986. 104p. bibliog.

As a non-OPEC oil producer, the Congo has seen significant changes resulting from the development of its petroleum resources and the instability of oil prices in recent times. This ILO report examines the social and economic results of such development on a worldwide basis.

345 **Petroleum company operations and agreements in the developing world.**
Raymond F. Mikesell. Washington, DC: Resources for the Future, 1984. 148p. bibliog.

Distributed by Johns Hopkins University Press, this research paper outlines the inter-relationship of the petroleum industry and national governments in the Third World and related government policies and financial issues. This provides an excellent background for studying the Congo's ties to foreign oil companies.

346   The mineral industry of Republic of the Congo (Brazzaville).
Thomas G. Murdock.   In: *Minerals Yearbook*. Washington, DC: US
Bureau of Mines, 1963. p. 881-88.

A good overview of mining in the Congo is offered in this work. Subsequent annual
issues of this US government publication offer additional facts and figures.

347   **Petrole Français.** (French Petroleum.)
Bernard Pierre.   Paris: Hachette, 1960. 265p. maps.

Accompanied by maps, diagrams and other illustrations, this account of the French oil
industry focuses on activities in former French African colonies. Although the subject
matter covered is for the period prior to the exploitation of petroleum in the Congo, it
offers valuable background material on some of the French interests which have
become active in the country.

348   **Electrical power supply, Loutété-Niari sector, Congo Republic.**
E. S. Preston, (et al.).   Washington, DC: USAID, 1964. 4 vols. maps.

This important, but dated report is concerned with the electrical power facilities
between the Congolese capital of Brazzaville and the country's only major port,
Pointe-Noire. This extensive report, which is illustrated and contains numerous maps,
is divided into four volumes: I, evaluation report; II, the economic and agricultural
development of the Niari valley; III, electric power supply in the Loutété-Niari sector;
and IV, exhibits and plans.

349   **Loudima water supply, Congo Republic: evaluation report and English
language abstract.**
E. S. Preston, (et al.).   Washington, DC: USAID, 1964. various
paginations.

Immediately following Congolese independence, the United States sponsored a
number of studies on the municipal and other public water supply facilities of the new
nation. Four studies were published in 1964, in which water resources and supply
facilities were described and future (mainly technical) courses of action were
recommended. This report concerns the Congo-Océan railway town of Loudima on the
Niari River. See also items no 350-52.

350   **Project of drinking water supply for Makoua, Congo Republic:
evaluation report and English language abstract.**
E. S. Preston, (et al.).   Washington, DC: USAID, 1964. various
paginations.

This is an American water supply study on Makoua, an important transport centre in
the north of the Cuvette region on the road to northern Gabon and Cameroon.

351   **Water supply for Kinkala, Congo Republic: evaluation report and
English language abstract.**
E. S. Preston, (et al.).   Washington, DC: USAID, 1964. various
paginations.

An American water supply study for Kinkala, the first major town on the railway and
road linking Brazzaville with Pointe-Noire.

352 **Water supply on Koukouya Plateau, Congo Republic: evaluation report and English language abstract.**
E. S. Preston, (et al.). Washington, DC: USAID, 1964. various paginations.

An American water supply study for the Koukouya Plateau region between Djambala and the Gabonese border.

353 **World petroleum resources and reserves.**
Joseph P. Riva. Boulder, Colorado: Westview, 1983. 355p.

This overview of global petroleum resources places the Congo in its world context as a minor producer.

354 **Industrialisierung in Aquatorialafrika.** (Industrialization in equatorial Africa.)
Eike W. Schamp. Munich: Weltforum-Verlag, 1978. 321p. maps. bibliog.

Issues related to the development of industries in the Congo, Gabon and Cameroon are examined in this German-language work, which contains numerous illustrated descriptions of industries.

355 **Tax and contractual arrangements for the exploitation of natural resources.**
Arvind Virmani. Washington, DC: World Bank, 1985. 139p. (World Bank Staff Working Paper no. 752).

This report examines the arrangements between corporations and governments for the exploitation of natural resources. Particular attention is paid to the development of petroleum reserves in developing countries, including the Congo.

Area handbook for the People's Republic of the Congo (Congo Brazzaville).
See item no. 3.

Bulletin de l'Afrique Noire. (Bulletin of Black Africa.)
See item no. 302.

Europe France Outre-mer. (Europe France Overseas.)
See item no. 308.

Le Moniteur Africain. (The African Monitor.)
See item no. 317.

L'Observateur Africain. (The African Observer.)
See item no. 319.

Colonialisme, néo-colonialism et la transition au capitalisme: exemple de la 'Comilog' au Congo-Brazzaville. (Colonialism, neo-colonialism and the transition to capitalism: the example of 'Comilog' in the Congo-Brazzaville.)
See item no. 320.

Bulletin Quotidien de l'ACI. (Daily bulletin of the ACI.)
See item no. 482.

Etumba. (Star.)
See item no. 485.

Jeune Afrique. (Young Africa.)
See item no. 489.

La Semaine. (The Week.)
See item no. 495.

Cahiers d'Outre-mer. (Overseas Notes.)
See item no. 517.

The Congo.
See item no. 521.

Encyclopedia of the Third World.
See item no. 523.

Agriculture

356 **African agrarian systems.**
Edited by Daniel Biebuyck.   London: Oxford University Press, 1963.
407p.
Biebuyck's collection on African agriculture contains a good deal of material on the
Congo, as well as relevant general information.

357 **Recherche de la densité optimale du palmier de huile planté en allées.**
(Research on the optimum density of oil palms planted in rows.)
R. E. Guldentorps, L. Scuvie.   Brussels: Institut pour l'Etude
Agronomique du Congo, 1968. [n.p.]
After the slave trade was abolished, palm oil became one of the most lucrative
commodities of the equatorial region of Africa. This Belgian study on maximizing oil
palm yields is applicable to the Congo, Zaïre and other Atlantic coastal areas of
tropical Africa.

358 **Small farm development: understanding and improving farming systems
in the humid tropics.**
Richard R. Harwood.   Boulder, Colorado: Westview, 1979. 160p.
This much-needed study of small farm improvement was sponsored by the
International Agricultural Development Service and contains much information which
is of use to agriculturalists, researchers and planners in the Congo.

359 **Food crops of the lowland tropics.**
Edited by C. L. A. Leakey, J. B. Wills.   Oxford: Oxford University
Press, 1977. 345p. maps. bibliog.
This reference work on tropical food crops concentrates on west Africa, but includes
much material applicable to the Congo.

360 Agriculture in the Congo Basin: tradition and change in African rural economies.
Marvin P. Miracle. Madison, Wisconsin: University of Wisconsin Press, 1967. 355p. maps. bibliog.
Accompanied by maps and other illustrations, this is a comprehensive look at agriculture along the Congo River. Important bibliographical references are included.

361 Agriculture and rural development in the People's Republic of the Congo.
Edited by Gregory Tien Hung Nguyen. Boulder, Colorado: Westview, 1986. 236p. bibliog.
Congolese agriculture, rural development and government economic policies are examined in great detail in this work, unique in the English language as a recent overview. Some illustrations are included.

362 Cocoa production: economic and botanical perspectives.
Edited by John Simmons. New York: Praeger, 1976. 413p.
A collection of essays and lectures on the economics and development of cocoa production and trade in Latin America and Africa, including the Congo.

363 Food production in a land-surplus, labor-scarce economy: the Zaïrean Basin.
Tshikala B. Tshibaka. Washington, DC: International Food Policy Research Institute, 1989. 70p.
Looking at the economic aspects of agriculture on both sides of the Congo (Zaïre) River, the author of this study is particularly concerned with the supply of and demand for agricultural labourers.

364 Cocoa.
G. A. R. Wood, R. A. Lass. London: Longman, 1985. 620p. bibliog.
This work is the chief reference in English on cacao cultivation and cocoa production. In the Congo, the cultivation of cacao expanded from its introduction in the Souanké district in 1947 until the late 1960s when the Congolese government's promotion of industrialization led to the neglect of the agricultural sector. Currently the north of the country continues to dominate national production, which has fallen to 2,000 tonnes per annum.

365 Agriculture in the tropics.
C. C. Webster, P. N. Wilson. London: Longman, 1980. 640p. bibliog. (Tropical Agriculture Series).
This is one of the best general texts available in English on tropical agriculture. An analysis of crops and techniques is accompanied by illustrations and a forty-page bibliography.

Congo: profile.
See item no. 1.

Agriculture

Area handbook for the People's Republic of the Congo (Congo Brazzaville).
See item no. 3.

Le Moniteur Africain. (The African monitor.)
See item no. 317.

Bulletin Quotidien de l'ACI. (Daily bulletin of the ACI.)
See item no. 482.

Jeune Afrique. (Young Africa.)
See item no. 489.

Cahiers d'Outre-mer. (Overseas notes.)
See item no. 517.

Encyclopedia of the Third World.
See item no. 523.

Forestry

366 Tropical forests, some African and Asian case studies of composition and structure.
Jan Borota. Amsterdam, New York: Elsevier, 1991. 274p. bibliog.
Translated from the Slovak, this reference on tropical rain forest analysis and management contains much useful material on the forest belt which includes much of the northern Congo.

367 Forest resources of tropical Africa.
Food and Agriculture Organization. Rome: FAO, 1981. 2 vols. (UN 32/6.1301-78-04, Technical Report no. 2).
Volume one of this work is a synthesis of regional information on forestry and forest products in tropical Africa. Volume two is divided into individual country reports, including one on the Congo. Bibliographical notes are included.

368 Forest pricing and concession policies: managing the high forest of west and central Africa.
Mikael Grut, John A. Gray, Nicolas Egli. Washington, DC: World Bank, 1991. 77p. bibliog. (World Bank Technical Paper no. 143).
This report looks at the economic aspects of forestry and government forestry policies throughout west and central Africa. More specific, but difficult to acquire, related information on the conditions for forestry exploitation in the Congo can be found in the Malian French language publication *L'Essor* (Progress), (25 Jan. 1969).

Forestry

369 **Essences forestieres et bois du Congo.** (Forest essences and wood in the Congo.)
Jean Louis, Joseph Fouarge.   Brussels: Institut National pour l'Etude Agronomique du Congo, 1953. various paginations. maps. bibliog.

This collection of information on forest products in Zaïre has direct relevance to the Congo where similar commodities are also being exploited. Arranged by product, this work includes many illustrations, maps, diagrams and bibliographical references.

Congo: profile.
See item no. 1.

Etude sur les fôrets d' Afrique Equatoriale Française et du Cameroun. (A study on the forests of French Equatorial Africa and Cameroon.)
See item no. 49.

Les bois du Gabon. (The forests of Gabon.)
See item no. 51.

Bois du Congo. (Wood of the Congo.)
See item no. 54.

Bulletin de l'Afrique noire. (Bulletin of Black Africa.)
See item no. 302.

Europe France Outre-mer. (Europe France Overseas.)
See item no. 308.

L'Observateur Africain. (The African Observer.)
See item no. 319.

Jeune Afrique. (Young Africa.)
See item no. 489.

Labour

Colonial

370 **The black man's burden: African colonial labor on the Congo and Ubangi rivers 1880-1900.**
William J. Samarin. Boulder, Colorado: Westview, 1989. 276p. bibliog.
The wealth of the Congo basin and the region's under-population have been sources of great difficulties past and present. Under French and Belgian colonialism, plans to exploit the basin were accompanied by serious abuses of the African labour force. This recent book examines indigenous labour along the Congo and Ubangi rivers ranging from the suppression of slavery and the introduction of colonial labour policies to the protests over and investigations into abuses in both the French and Belgian Congos.

Post-colonial

371 **Congo Brazzaville: industrial relations under the new labour code.**
Inter-African Labour Institute. *Inter-African Labour Institute Information Sheet* (Bamako, Mali), vol. 6, no. 5 (Oct. 1964), p. 2, 9.
This explanation of the Congo's 1964 labour code contains material on the Congolese appenticeship system, trade unions and industrial relations.

372 **Inter-African Labour Institute Bulletin.**
Bamako, Mali: Inter-African Labour Institute, 1954-65. bimonthly
(1954-60), quarterly (1960-5).

Articles of interest include: M. R. Devauges' 'Unemployment in Brazzaville', vol. 7,
no. 3 (May 1960). p. 8-49; an unattributed article entitled 'General structure of social
security systems in French-speaking African states: Congo (Brazzaville), Guinea, Ivory
Coast and Congo (Léopoldville)' vol. 9, no. 2 (May 1962), p. 31-65; and Louis-Koffi
Amega's 'A Sociological study of factors of juvenile delinquency in Congo-Brazzaville'
vol. 11, no. 2 (May 1964). p. 214.

Bulletin Quotidien de l'ACI. (Daily bulletin of the ACI.)
See item no. 482.

Etumba. (Star.)
See item no. 485.

Statistics

373 **Current national statistical compendiums.**
Congressional Information Service.   Washington, DC: CIS, 1980-.
microfiches.

In the series Africa and North and Central America, the Congo appears as item 12 (mistakenly labelled as Zaïre) in this microfilmed collection of various statistics which is updated annually for both governmental and public use.

374 **Bulletin Mensuel Statistique.** (Monthly statistical bulletin.)
Brazzaville: Direction de la Statistique et de la Comptabilité
Économique, 1958-1976. monthly.

Official economic and social statistics were provided by this publication, originally set up by the French colonial administration.

375 **Bulletin de Statistique.** (Statistical bulletin.)
Brazzaville: Centre Nationale de la Statistique et des Etudes
Économiques, 1977-. quarterly.

This quarterly succeeded the previous entry.

Area handbook for the People's Republic of the Congo (Congo Brazzaville).
See item no. 3.

Congo, Gabon, Equatorial Guinea: country report, analyses of economic and political trends.
See item no. 311.

Congo: country profile, annual survey of political and economic background.
See item no. 312.

Statistics

Quarterly review of Gabon, Congo, Cameroon, the Central African Republic, Chad and Equatorial Guinea.
See item no. 313.

Annual report.
See item no. 314.

Foreign economic trends and their implications for the United States: Congo.
See item no. 324.

Etudes et statistiques de la BEAC. (Studies and statistics of the Bank of Central African States.)
See item no. 326.

The Congo.
See item no. 521.

A historical dictionary of the People's Republic of the Congo.
See item no. 526.

Education

376 **Annales.** (Annals.)
     Brazzaville: University of Brazzaville, 1970-. annual.
University affairs, educational programmes and research projects are the main subjects
of this annual. There have been a number of other journals related to education in the
Congo, including the University of Brazzaville's *Dimi*, a journal of language (June
1973-); and *Mbongui*, the educational, psychological and sociological journal of the
Institut Superieur des Sciences de l'Education, both of which have been irregular.

377 **Schooling in the states of equatorial Africa.**
     David E. Gardinier. *Canadian Journal of African Studies*, vol. 8, no.
     3 (1974), p. 517-38.
Gardinier, the leading expert on education in equatorial Africa provides a good
introduction to the educational system of the Congo in this article.

378 **Education in French Equatorial Africa, 1842-1945.**
     David E. Gardinier. *Proceedings of the French Colonial Historical
     Society*, vol. 3 (1978), p. 121-37.
A good, but brief, historical survey of education in French Equatorial Africa during
the colonial period.

Education

379   **Histoire et organisation générale de l'enseignement en Afrique**
       Equatoriale Française. (History and general organization of education
       in French Equatorial Africa.)
       Office of the Governor-General.   Brazzaville: Imprimerie Officielle,
       1931. 97p.
An official view of education in French Equatorial Africa during the inter-war years.

380   **Trends in Congolese education described.**
       Henri Lopès.   *US Joint Publications Research Service Translations on*
       Africa (Washington, DC), no. 724 (1968), p. 75-82.
Lopès introduces the post-colonial Congolese educational system in this translation of
his article which first appeared in *L'Obserateur Africain*, vol. 7, (May-June 1968),
p. 63-7.

381   **Formal education in the Congo-Brazzaville.**
       Gerard Lucas.   Stanford, California: Comparative Education Center
       (Stanford University), 1964. 287p.
Based on the author's PhD dissertation at Stanford University, this 'study of
educational policy and practice' was supported by the Co-operative Research Program
of the US Office of Education (Co-operative Research Project no. 1032). It describes
the Congolese school system and analyses education as an instrument of national
policy.

382   **Selected French-speaking Sub-Saharan African countries: Burundi,**
       Cameroon (Eastern), Chad, Congo (Brazzaville), Dahomey, Gabon,
       Ivory Coast, Mali, Mauritania, Niger, Rwanda, Senegal, Togo, Upper
       Volta and Zaïre.
       Edouard J. C. Trudeau.   Washington, DC: Educational Resources
       Information Center (ERIC), 1975. 20p. on 1 microfiche card.
       (Document no. ED 249900).
Sub-titled 'a guide to the academic placement of students from these countries in
academic institutions of the United States' this work provides a description of the
educational system of the Congo and fourteen other African nations and is designed
for American university officials to assess the needs of students from Francophone
Africa. ERIC is a division of the Office of Educational Research and Improvement of
the US Department of Education, which compiles and provides specialized information
related to education and social development.

Area handbook for the People's Republic of the Congo (Congo Brazzaville).
See item no. 3.

Le Moniteur Africain. (The African monitor.)
See item no. 317.

Bulletin Quotidien de l'ACI. (Daily bulletin of the ACI.)
See item no. 482.

116

Etumba. (Star.)
See item no. 485.

La Semaine. (The Week.)
See item no. 495.

Bulletin de l'Institut de Recherches Scientifiques au Congo. (Bulletin of the Institute for Scientific Research in the Congo.)
See item no. 515.

The Congo.
See item no. 521.

Encyclopedia of the Third World.
See item no. 523.

Education in the states of equatorial Africa: a bibliographical essay.
See item no. 531.

Literature

383 **L'Homme qui tua la crocodile: tragicomédie.** (The man who killed the crocodile: a tragicomedy.)
Sylvain Bemba.   Yaoundé, Cameroon: Éditions CLE, 1972. 72p.

This play in French by Sylvain Bemba, who has become widely regarded as one of the most talented Congolese authors past and present, is about a tyrant who mistreats his wife and people and is challenged by the local schoolteacher, symbolizing the multi-level conflict between education and injustice. Bemba is one of many Congolese writers who have been in government service. He was director of the Congo's press agency (Agence Congolaise d'Information – ACI), director of radio and television broadcasting, director-general of information, director-general of cultural affairs and minister of information. Out of favour after 1973, he has continued to write, sometimes using the pseudonyms Martial Malinda (see item no. 405) and Michel Belvain. Bemba's most important other works are *Une eau dormante* (A still water) (Paris: Radio-France Internationale, 1975. 103p), a French-language play, set in the 1930s, which deals with the issues faced by an individual who defies tradition; *Tarentelle noire et diable blanc* (Black tarantula and white devil) (Paris: P.J. Oswald, 1976. 136p), a French-language play in which Bemba looks at the abuses of French colonialism in the Congo from 1890 to 1930 through the eyes of a Congolese named Ibouanga and his family; *Un foutu monde pour un blanchisseur trop honnête* (A dirty world for a too honest washerman) (Yaoundé, Cameroon: Éditions C.L.E., 1979. 48p), a play, written in French, but with much pidgin usage which examines honesty in a world where, according to the author, 'dishonesty is normal'.; *Rêves portatifs* (Portable dreams) (Dakar: Nouvelles Éditions Africaines, 1979. 208p), Bemba's first novel which deals with disillusionment and the souring of many of Africa's post-independence dreams.; and *Le soleil est parti à M'Pemba* (The sun is gone to M'Pemba) (Paris: Présence Africaine, 1982. 186p), a novel.

384 **Bio-bibliographie des ecrivains Congolais.** (A bio-bibliography of
   Congolese writers.)
   S. Bemba, L. P. Mamonsono.   Brazzaville: Éditions Litteraires
   Congolaises, 1979. 33p.

This short French-language reference work provides a list of Congolese authors, their
works and biographical details.

385 **Témoignages.** (Memories.)
   Jean-Blaise Bilombo-Samba.   Paris: Oswald, 1976. 85p.

Bilombo-Samba's first book of verse contains a preface by Henri Lopès.

386 **Chômeur à Brazzaville.** (Unemployed in Brazzaville.)
   Pierre Biniakounou.   Dakar: Nouvelles Éditions Africaines, 1977.
   78p.

This is a short novel about joblessness and misery in the slums of Brazzaville, written
in French.

387 **African literature in French.**
   Dorothy S. Blair.   Cambridge, England; New York: Cambridge
   University Press, 1976. 348p.

Described as 'a history of creative writing in French from west and equatorial Africa',
Blair's book is a good reference work on the literature of the Congo and other
Francophone African nations.

388 **Wit and wisdom from West Africa.**
   Richard F. Burton.   New York: Negro University Press, 1969. 455p.

Described as 'a book of proverbial philosophy, idioms, enigmas and laconisms',
Burton's collection includes a number of Fang proverbs and idiomatic usages which
reveal something of the philosophy, society and worldview of the inhabitants of
western equatorial Africa.

389 **Whispers from a continent: the literature of contemporary black Africa.**
   Edited by Wilfred Cartey.   New York: Random House & Vintage,
   1969; London: Heinemann, 1971. 397p.

Congolese author Jean Malonga is included in this survey of African writing. Entries
are grouped by theme.

390 **Panorama critique de la litterature Congolaise contemporaine.** (A
   critical panorama of comtemporary Congolese literature.)
   Roger Chemain, Arlette Chemain-Degrange.   Paris: Présence
   Africaine, 1979. 237p. bibliog.

The history of French-language literature in the Congo is examined in this critical
work, which includes a four-page bibliography.

Literature

391 **Africa in prose.**
Edited by O. R. Dathorne, W. Feuser   Harmondsworth, England:
Penguin, 1969. 384p.

This collection of forty-four extracts from modern African literature includes work by
Jean Malonga and is accompanied by commentaries and biographical notes.

392 **African poetry for schools and colleges.**
Edited by O. R. Dathorne   London: Macmillan, 1969. 166p.

This collection, which includes work by G. F. Tchicaya U Tam'si, successfully
illustrates the many forms of African verse. Oral poetry, verse in African vernacular
languages and both early and contemporary works in English and French are all
included. The second section of the book comprises extensive notes on both the works
and their authors.

393 **Voix d'Afrique: echos du monde.** (Voice of Africa: echoes in the
world.)
Edited by Ekoa M. Diboti, Richard Dogbeh.   Paris: Institute
Pédagogique Africaine et Malgache, 1965. 256p.

This illustrated textbook for primary schools in Francophone Africa uses extracts from
African and French novels and poetry to illustrate scenes from everyday life on the
African continent. Among the featured writings are those of Congolese Jean Malonga.

394 **Un fusil dans la main, un poème dans la poche.** (A gun in the hand, a
poem in the pocket.)
Emmanuel-Boundzeki Dongala.   Paris: Albin Michel, 1973. 284p.

The transformation of a young revolutionary into his country's leader and the realities
of African politics are related in this excellent novel in French. In 1974 this work
created a stir in the Congo and is particularly remarkable in that Dongala is an
American- and French-educated chemistry professor at the University of Brazzaville,
whose first love is literature. His more recent works include *Jazz et vin de palme et
autre nouvelles* (Jazz and palm wine and other stories) (Paris: Hatier, 1982. 156p), a
collection of short stories in French; and *Le feu des origines* (The authentic fires)
(Paris: Albin Michel, 1987. 255p), a novel.

395 **Anthologie Africaine et Malgache.** (An African and Malagasy
anthology.)
Edited by Langston Hughes, Christiane Reynault.   Paris: Seghers,
1962. 307p.

Among the short stories, essays and poems of this French-language anthology is work
by Congolese poet Martial Sinda.

396 **Poems from black Africa.**
Edited by Langston Hughes.   Bloomington, Indiana: Indiana
University Press, 1966. 158p.

Although emphasizing Anglophone African writers, Hughes also includes work by
G. F. Tchicaya U Tam'si in this anthology.

397 **Anthologie Africaine des écrivains noirs d'expression Française.** (An
African anthology of black writers of French expression.)
Edited by André Justin.   Paris: Institute Pédagogique Africaine, 1962.
190p.

The work of Jean Malonga is featured in this collection of prose works by major
French-language African writers.

398 **Anthologie négro-Africaine: panorama critique des prosateurs, poètes et
dramatourges noires du XXème siecle.** (A black African anthology: a
critical panorama of 20th century black prose writers, poets and
playwrights.)
Edited by Lilyan Kesteloot.   Verviers, Belgium: Gérard, 1967. 432p.

This comprehensive French-language survey of black authors from Africa, the
Caribbean and the Americas includes work by Jean Malonga and G. F. Tchicaya U
Tam'si. Biographical notes and illustrations accompany the text.

399 **Les conjurés du 17 janvier 1961.** (The conspirators of 17 January 1961.)
Noël-Ramatta Kodia.   Brazzaville: Héros dans l'Ombre, [n.d.]. 39p.

In this left wing play in French, Africa brings suit against Europe and her sons East
and West for the death of Patrice Lumumba in a trial presided over by judges Asia and
Latin America.

400 **L'Europe inculpée: drame en quatre actes.** (Europe accused: a drama in
four acts.)
Antoine Letembet-Ambily.   Yaoundé, Cameroon: CLE, 1977. 116p.

In this drama, the Biblical character of Noah returns to earth to testify before the
judge Humanity when Europe and America (daughter and granddaughter of Noah's
son Japheth) are accused of exploiting Africa (daughter of Noah's son Ham.) A
similarly themed work of Letembet-Ambily is *Les aryens: tragédie en trois actes* (The
aryans: a tragedy in three acts) (Yaoundé, Cameroon: CLE, 1977. 60p). Letembet-
Ambily's symbolic attacks on racism and fascism in these plays seem to be tainted with
both naïvety and a measure of anti-white racism.

401 **Tribaliques.** (Tribalics.)
Henri Lopès.   Yaoundé, Cameroon: CLE, 1971. 104p.

This excellent collection of eight short stories in French points out the ironies,
dilemmas, hypocrisies and other social and political issues in contemporary Africa.
Lopès has served as the Congo's minister of education, foreign minister, prime
minister, director of the PCT newspaper and minister of finance and as the deputy
director-general of UNESCO. His other work includes *La nouvelle romance* (The new
romance) (Yaoundé, Cameroon: CLE, 1976; Dakar: Nouvelles Éditions Africaines,
1980. 196p), a French-language novel of the liberation of an African woman, Wali,
from exploitation by her husband, traced through the Congo and Europe; and *Sans
tam-tam* (Without tom-tom) (Yaoundé, Cameroon: CLE, 1977. 126p), Lopès' second
novel in French, which reveals the letters of a young schoolteacher who dies after
returning to his village school to serve his people rather than taking a diplomatic
posting in Paris.

402 **Balbutiements.** (Stammerings.)
Enoch Mabassi. Brazzaville: Héros dans L'Ombre, 1977. 90p.
A poetry collection in French.

403 **Boutou grand soir: poèmes affiches.** (Great Boutou night: poster
poems.)
Auguste Macouba. Paris: Éditions Saint-Germain-des-Prés, 1978.
43p.
A collection of political poetry in French.

404 **En quête de la liberté: ou une vie d'espoir.** (In search of liberty: or a life
of hope.)
Jean-Pierre Makouta-Mboukou. Yaoundé, Cameroon: CLE, 1970.
168p.
This French-language book is the coming of age story of a young man who experiences
family deaths, injustice, racism, friendship, political reality and exile. His other works
are *Les initiés* (The initiates) (Yaoundé, Cameroon: CLE, 1970. 88p.), a story of tragic
love; *L'ame-bleue: poèmes* (The blue spirit: poems) (Yaoundé, Cameroon: CLE,
1971. 112p.), a collection of French-language poetry; *Le contestant* (The contestant)
(Paris: La Pensée Universelle, 1973. 256p.), a novel of adulterous love, religious
atonement and tragedy in French; *Cantate d' l'ouvrier* (Worker's cantata) (Paris:
Oswald, 1974. 70p.), a collection of political poetry in French; and *Les exilés de la forêt
viérge ou le grand complot* (The exiles of the virgin forest or the great conspiracy)
(Paris: Oswald, 1974. 210p.), Makouta-Mboukou's fourth novel in French, in which a
deposed president of an imaginary African nation and a poet whom he had condemned
to death meet and are reconciled in the forest of their country of exile.

405 **L'Enfer c'est Orféo: pièce en trois actes.** (Hell is Orféo: a play in three
acts.)
Martial Malinda. Paris: ORTF-DAEC, 1970. 120p.
Writing under the pseudonym Martial Malinda, Congolese playwright Sylvain Bemba
depicts the transformations experienced by a rich doctor during the struggle for
independence in Guinea-Bissau.

406 **La légende de M'Pfoumou ma Mazono.** (The legend of M'Pfoumou ma
Mazono.)
Jean Malonga. Paris: Présence Africaine, 1973. 153p.
In this prize-winning French-language novel, adultery followed by war and flight
comprise the background of the birth of a great chief who abolishes slavery and other
traditional forms of injustice. Malonga's other noteworthy work is *Coeur d'aryenne*
(Heart of the Aryan) (Paris: Présence Africaine, 1955).

407 **Light-Houses.**
Léopold P. Mamonsono. Brazzaville: Héros dans l'Ombre, 1978. 52p.
Poems in English in which Mamonsono evokes his ancestral Congo and his citizenship
in the modern world. He has also written several works in French, including *Héros
dans l'ombre* (Hero of the darkness) (Brazzaville: Éditions Littéraires Congolaises,

1976. 48p.), a collection of poems dedicated to teachers; *Luzingu-Lua-Liadi: une vie d'enfer* (Luzingu-Lua-Liadi: a life of hell) (Brazzaville: Héros dans l'Ombre, 1976. 138p.), a short novel; *Mutantu: ou la tragédie de l'enfant naturel* (Mutantu: or the tragedy of the natural child) (Brazzaville: Héros dans l'Ombre, 1976. 150p.), an autobiographical novel; *Tembe na Mundele Alongui: malheur d'Irace* (Tembe na Mundele Alongui: misfortune of Irace) (Brazzaville: Héros dans l'Ombre, 1977. 253p.), a novel described as a 'social tragedy'; and *Le regard du fou* (The madman's look) (Dakar: Nouvelles Africaines, 1981. various paginations), a play.

408 **La nouvelle generation de poetes Congolais.** (The new generation of Congolese poets.)
   Léopold P. Mamonsono.   Brazzaville: Kivouvou, 1984. 228p.
This book is a good introduction to the modern, largely left-wing, poets of the Congo during its period of experimentation with Marxism.

409 **Echo.**
   Manki Man Tséké.   Paris: Oswald, 1977. 54p.
Poetry in French by a Congolese writer.

410 **La marmite de Koka-Mbala: pièce en deux actes.** (The pot of Koka-Mbala: a play in two acts.)
   Guy Menga.   Monaco: Regain, 1966; Yaoundé, Cameroon: CLE, 1976. 96p.
Guy Menga, pseudonym for Gaston-Guy Bikouta-Menga, writes of a conflict between justice and traditional order in this early play in French. The 1976 edition of this work also includes *L'Oracle* (see item no. 412).

411 **La palabre stérile.** (Fruitless palavers.)
   Guy Menga.   Yaoundé, Cameroon: CLE, 1968. 138p.
Awarded the Grand Prix Littéraire de l'Afrique Noire in 1969, Menga's short novel in French traces the events and changes in the life of a young Congolese who leaves his native village on the eve of independence. The volume is part of CLE's *Collection Abbia.*

412 **L'Oracle: comédie en trois actes.** (The oracle: a comedy in three acts.)
   Guy Menga.   Paris: ORTF-DAEC, 1969. 90p.
A daughter who wishes to continue her studies and her father who wants her to marry a rich old man are brought to an agreement by a grandfather in this award-winning French-language play by Menga.

413 **Les indiscrétions du vagabond: contes et récits du Congo.** (The indiscretions of the vagabond: tales and stories of the Congo.)
   Guy Menga.   Sherbrooke, Canada: Naaman, 1974. 96p.
Seven traditional and four contemporary tales are presented by a traveller who entertains a Congolese village for six nights in this cleverly structured book in French by Guy Menga.

Literature

414 **Les aventures de Moni-Mambou.** (The adventures of Moni-Mambou.)
Guy Menga.   Yaoundé, Cameroon: CLE, 1975. 126p.

Accompanied by his talking parrot Yengui, the Congolese folk hero Moni-Mambou fights evil and defends the oppressed. Originally published in 1971, further stories were published in 1975 as *Les nouvelles aventures de Moni-Mambou* (The new adventures of Moni-Mambou) and *Les aventures de Moni-Mambou 3* (The adventures of Moni-Mambou 3). This edition includes the first two of this series and the third is available separately (Yaoundé: CLE, 1975. 64p.). The first book in this series was also translated into English by Malachy Quinn as *The adventures of Moni-Mambou* (London: Evans, 1979).

415 **Kotawali.** (Great woman.)
Guy Menga.   Dakar: Nouvelles Africaines, 1976. 288p.

The lives of a young female revolutionary, a taxi driver and his wife are entangled in this French-language novel, Menga's first.

416 **La soumission: roman Congolais.** (The submission: a Congolese romance.)
Dominique M'Fouillou.   Paris: L'Harmattan, 1977. 150p.

The hero of this novel, which critically examines colonialism, comes of age in the turbulent ten years from 1935 to 1945.

417 **Les corbeaux.** (The crows.)
Dominique M'Fouillou.   Le Mée-sur-Seine, France: Akpagnon, 1980. 240p.

The 'crows' in this French-language novel are the followers of André Matswa preparing to free the Congo from internal and external enemies.

418 **Surrealism and negritude in the poetry of Tchikaya U Tam'si.**
Gerald Moore.   *Black Orpheus*, no. 13 (Nov. 1963), p. 5-12.

Moore's article on G. F. Tchikaya U Tam'si describes the many influences on the Congolese poet, among them the writings of Aime Césairé, the arts and crafts of the Congo, the Surrealists and the concept of negritude.

419 **Time and experience in African poetry.**
Gerald Moore.   *Transition*, vol. 6, no. 26 (1966), p. 18-22.

Suggesting that traditional and modern African poetry convey a unique conception of time and space, this article includes examples from the poetry of G. F. Tchikaya U Tam'si among others.

420 **The negro poet and his landscape.**
Gerald Moore.   *Black Orpheus*, no. 22 (Aug. 1967), p. 35-38.

Tchikaya U Tam'si is the main focus of this article which explores his imagery and describes him as 'emerging as the outstanding poet of French expression among those who have been publishing since the war (World War II)'.

421 **Modern poetry from Africa.**
Edited by Gerald Moore, Ulli Beier.   Harmondsworth, England:
Penguin, 1968. 192p.

This popular anthology in English draws on the work of authors in sixteen African countries in three languages (English, French and Portuguese.) G. F. Tchicaya U Tam'si and J. B. Tatti-Loutard represent Congolese verse. Biographical notes on the authors and an index of first lines are included.

422 **N'Ganga Mayala: tragédie en trois actes.** (N'Ganga Mayala: a tragedy
in three acts.)
Ferdinand Mouangassa.   Yaoundé, Cameroon: CLE, 1977. 78p.

A traditional ruler's reforms end tragically in this French-language play about the realities of African politics.

423 **African writing today.**
Edited by Ezekiel Mphahlele.   Harmondsworth, England: Penguin,
1967. 347p.

This anthology is 'intended to give the intelligent reader a map of themes and styles of African writing in the metropolitan languages – English, French and Portuguese'. A wide sampling of literature from fifteen African countries is presented and translated into English. There are brief introductions and biographical notes on each author. Congolese authors include S. Bemba and G. F. Tchicaya U Tam'si.

424 **Soleils neufs.** (Nine suns.)
Maxime N'Debeka.   Yaoundé, Cameroon: CLE, 1969. 107p.

This collection of Congolese poetry is part of CLE's *Collection Abbia*. Other works of verse by N'Debeka include *L'Oseille et les citrons* (Sorrel and lemons) (Paris: Oswald, 1975. 70p.); and *Les signes du silence* (Signs of silence) (Paris: Saint-Germain-des-Prés, 1978. 57p.).

425 **Le président: drame satirique en trois actes.** (The president: a satirical
drama in three acts.)
Maxime N'Debeka.   Paris: Oswald, 1970. 95p.

A cynical African president is overthrown in this drama of political commentary in French. Prefaced by Henri Lopès.

426 **Le Mvett.** (The Mvet.)
Tsira Ndong Ndoutoume.   Paris: Présence Africaine, 1970. 157p.

A unique collection of Fang tales named after the guitar-like musical instrument favoured by the tribe.

427 **Lettre à un étudiant Africain. La sonate des derniers veilleurs.** (Letter
to an African student. The sonata of the last watchmen.)
Dominique Ngoie-Ngalla.   Brazzaville: Mbonda, 1981. 34p.

These two French-language short stories are really philosophical essays. The first expresses concern over selfishness, possible Arab domination of Africa and the possibility of combining revolutionary ideas and religious attitudes. The second story is a plea for Africa's maturity, an acceptance of her faults by her leaders and citizens and an end to the violence which afflicts the continent.

428 **Le Mvet: Un gengre littéraire Fang.** (The Mvet: a Fang literary genre.)
M. Nkoa ze Lecourt.   unpublished thesis. EPHE, Paris, 1973.

Popular among the Fang, the Mvet balladeers have religious and social (and more recently political) roles. This study in French examines their role and literary aspects.

429 **Deuxième bureau.** (Intelligence service.)
Alphonse Nkouka.   Yaoundé, Cameroon: CLE, 1980. 150p.

A novel on the tragic love affair of a single woman.

430 **Le tipoye doré: recit.** (The gilded sedan chair: a story.)
Placide N'Zala-Backa.   Paris: Oswald, 1976. 80p.

Africa from the colonial era to independence is seen by a youth, growing to adulthood and becoming a civil servant in this novella, first published in Brazzaville in 1968.

431 **Litterature traditionnelle des M'bochi.** (Traditional literature of the M'boshi.)
Theophile Obenga.   Paris: Présence Africaine, 1984. 325p.

Twelve pages of illustrations accompany this description of the folk literature of the M'boshi tribe of the northern Congo. Material is also included on other aspects of the group's customs and folklore. Obenga, an M'boshi himself, has led a distinguished career as a historian, writer and politician.

432 **Stèles pour l'avenir.** (Steles for the future.)
Théophile Obenga.   Paris: Présence Africaine, 1978. 79p.

This is a book of poetry in French by a Congolese who already distinguished himself as both professor of Egyptology at the University of Brazzaville and as foreign minister for nearly four years.

433 **La trilogie déterminante, Sélé-Sélé le mauvais cadre agricole, Tokolonga ou le socialisme triomphera.** (The decisive trilogy, Sélé-Sélé the bad agricultural cadre, Tokolonga or socialism triumphs.)
Owi-Okanza.   Bucharest, Romania: Ilexim, 1975. 138p.

These three plays, written in French by Owi-Okanza (pseudonym for Jacob Okanza) have a common Marxist theme of workers and peasants winning out against bureaucrats and expatriates. Continuing his hard line Marxist themes, Owi-Okanza also wrote *Oba l'instituteur, Les sangsues* (Oba the teacher, The leeches) (Bucharest, Romania: Ilexim, 1975. 189p.) two Marxist plays which portray the radicalization of a young African teacher drafted to fight in the Second World War and the corruption of an African politician who profits from colonialism. *Sélé-Sélé le Mauvais Cadre Agricole* and *Oba l'Instituteur* have been also published together by Présence Africaine.

434 **Présence Africaine.** (African Presence.)

Paris: 1947-. (English language edition 1961-8.) bimonthly (1947-55), quarterly (1955-).

The main literary journal of French-speaking Africa, Présence Africaine has published many works of Congolese authors. Of particular interest are the article 'Nouvelle somme de poésie du monde noir' (A New summary of poetry of the black world) (vol. 19, no. 57, Jan.-March 1966, p. 35-43) and Mwene Ndzale Obenga's 'Le Royaume de Makoko' (The Kingdom of Makoko) (vol. 22, no. 70, April-June 1969, p. 28-45).

435 **A book of African verse.**

Edited by John Reed, Clive Wake. London: Heinemann, 1964. 119p.

Among this anthology's thirty poets from eleven African countries is Congolese Martial Sinda. This book features a critical introduction; biographical and explanatory notes and an index of first lines.

436 **Proverbes Kongo.** (Kongo proverbs.)

Hubert van Roy. Tervuren, Belgium: Musée Royale de l'Afrique Centrale, 1963. 127p.

A collection of folk wisdom in French and Kikongo.

437 **Anthologie de la littérature négro-Africaine: romanciers et conteurs négro-Africains.** (An anthology of black African literature: black African novelists and story-tellers.)

Edited by Léonard Sainville. Paris: Présence Africaine, 1963 (vol. 1), 1968 (vol. 2). 456p. & 644p. respectively.

This two-volume anthology contains numerous extracts from the works of black African, Caribbean and North American writers, but places heavy emphasis on Francophone African literature. Selections of work by Jean Malonga are featured in Volume 1.

438 **Poèmes diplomatiques.** (Diplomatic poems.)

Eugène Sama. Paris: Oswald, 1976. 111p.

A collection of verse in French by a Congolese poet.

439 **Premier chant du départ.** (First song of the departure.)

Martial Sinda. Paris: Seghers, 1955. 61p.

An early poetry collection in French by a Congolese author, who around the time of this also the director of the PCT's newspaper *Etumba*.

440 **The African assertion: a critical anthology of African literature.**

Edited by Austin J. Shelton, Jr.. New York: Odyssey, 1968. 273p.

The poetry and prose extracts in this collection include Congolese work by G. F. Tchicaya U Tam'si and W. Tshakatumba.

441 **La vie et demie.** (Life and a half.)

Sony Labou Tansi.   Paris: du Seuil, 1979. 192p.

In this political fable in French, a brutal dictator is challenged by the prostitute daughter of one of his victim's. Tansi also wrote *L'Etat honteux* (The shameful state) (Paris: du Seuil, 1981. 160p.), a French-language novel on the absurdities of politics in some African states.

442 **Conscience de tracteur.** (Tractor conscience.)

Sony Labou Tansi.   Dakar: Nouvelles Éditions Africaines, 1979. 116p.

A mad scientist attempts to 'save' humanity through death and selective re-birth in this play by a Congolese author set in an imaginary central African nation. Introduced by Henri Lopès. Tansi's other major drama is *La parenthèse de sang* (The parenthesis of blood) (Paris: Hatier, 1981. 156p.).

443 **Poèmes de la mer.** (Poems of the sea.)

Jean-Baptiste Tatti-Loutard.   Yaoundé, Cameroon: CLE, 1969. 64p.

This short book of poetry, by a Congolese poet-politician is part of CLE's *Collection Abbia* and includes an essay on black poetry. Tatti-Loutard was minister of higher education (December 1975-April 1977) and later minister of arts, culture and sports in the 1980s. His other works, all in French, include *Les racines Congolaises* (Congolese roots) (Honfleur, France: P.J. Oswald, 1968. 77p.), a volume of verse accompanied by a critical essay entitled *La Vie Poétique*; *L'Envers du Soleil* (The wrong side of the sun) (Honfleur, France: Oswald, 1970. 69p.), Tatti-Loutard's third volume of poetry; *Les normes du temps* (The norms of the times) (Kinshasa, Zaïre: Éditions du Mont Noir, 1974. 70p.), his fourth book of verse; *Chroniques Congolaises: nouvelles* (Congolese chronicles: short stories) (Paris: Oswald, 1974. 135p.), collection of short stories; *Les feux de la planète* (The fires of the planet) (Dakar: Nouvelles Éditions Africaines, 1977. 41p.), another volume of poetry; and *Nouvelles Chroniques Congolaises* (New Congolese chronicles) (Paris: Présence Africaine, 1980. 188p.), a collection of twelve short stories in which the central theme is 'disappointment due to the irony of circumstances'.

444 **Feu de brousse.** (Brush fire.)

Gérald Félix Tchicaya U Tam'si.   Paris: Caractères, 1957. 86p.

The Congo's greatest literary figure has been poet Gérald Félix Tchicaya U Tam'si. This work, his most famous early book of verse, was also translated into English by Sangodare Akanji (pseud. for Ulli Beier) as *Brush Fire* (Ibadan: Mbari, 1964.) However, the original in French is much easier to find. Tchicaya's other early poetic works are *Le mauvais sang* (Bad blood) (Paris: Caractères, 1955. 45p.), Tchicaya U Tam'si's first published collection of verse and *À triche coeur* (Cheated heart) (Paris: Éditions Hautefeuille, 1958. 82p.). *Feu de Brousse*, *Le Mauvais Sang* and *A Triche-Coeur* were reissued as a single volume by P. J. Oswald in 1970 and again by Harmattan in 1978.

445 **Légendes Africaines.** (African legends.)

Edited by Gérald Félix Tchicaya U Tam'si.   Paris: Séghers, 1969. 264p.

The first of this collection of fourteen African legends and folk tales is provided by Tchicaya U Tam'si, who also edited and introduced this work.

446 **Selected poems.**
Gérald Félix Tchicaya U Tam'si. London: Heinemann, 1970. 143p.

Translated from the French by Gerald Moore, this sampling of Tchicaya U Tam'si's poetry includes *Brush Fire* (see item no. 444) and other works published in French throughout the 1950s and 1960s. However, these selections offer only a taste of this accomplished Congolese writer's work. The overwhelming majority of his writings have been in French. Originally published in 1962, Tchicaya U Tam'si's fourth book of verse was *Epitomé* (Epitome) (Honfleur, France: Oswald, 1968. 137p.) His importance is amply illustrated by this volume's introduction by Senegalese President Léopold Sédar Senghor. A collection named *Le ventre* (The belly) (Paris: Présence Africaine, 1964. 136p.) won Tchicaya U Tam'si first prize for poetry at the first World Festival of Negro Arts in Dakar in 1966. In 1978 Présence Africaine reissued this work along with two new poems, collectively entitled *Le Pain ou la Cendre*. Other works of verse in French have included *L'arc musical* (The musical bow) (Honfleur, France: Oswald, 1969. 172p.), a collection of Tchicaya U Tam'si's verse which also includes *Epitomé*; and *La veste d'intérieur* (The inner jacket) (Paris: Nubia, 1977. 111p.), more award-winning verse by Tchicaya.

447 **Le destin glorieux du Maréchal Nnikon Nniku, prince qu'on sort: comédie-farce-sinistre en trois plans.** (The glorious destiny of Marshal Nnikon Nniku, prince of destiny: a comedy-farce-disaster on three levels.)
Gérald Félix Tchicaya U Tam'si. Paris: Présence Africaine, 1979. 112p.

A pun-filled satirical drama on African dictatorships. This play was also translated into English as *The Glorious Destiny of Marshal Nnikon Nniku* by the Ubu Repertory Theater of New York in 1986. Another of Tchicaya's dramatic works is *Le Zulu* (The Zulu) (Paris: Nubia, 1977. 149p.), a volume of two plays, of which the title piece is a version of the story of Zulu leader Chaka. One of his most recent plays is *Les Phalenes* (The moths) (Paris: Albin Michel, 1984. 250p.).

448 **Les cancrelats.** (The cockroaches.)
Gérald Félix Tchicaya U Tam'si. Paris: Albin Michel, 1980. 320p.

Tchicaya U Tam'si's first novel deals with the disappointing conditions of contemporary African society.

449 **La main sèche.** (The dry hand.)
Gérald Félix Tchicaya U Tam'si. Paris: Laffont, 1980. 208p.

A collection of eleven short stories examining a variety of subjects, including African messianic leaders and pompous social gatherings.

450 **The madman and the medusa.**
Gérald Félix Tchicaya U Tam'si. Charlottesville, Virginia: University Press of Virginia, 1989. 213p.

An English-language edition of 'Meduses, ou, Les Orties de Mer' translated from the French by Sonja Haussmann Smith and William J. Smith with an introduction by Eric Sellin. Tchicaya's other recent work is *Ces fruits si doux de l'arbre à pain* (Paris: Séghers, 1987. 327p.).

Literature

451 **Longue est la nuit.** (Long is the night.)
Tchichellé Tchivéla.   Paris: Hatier, 1980. 127p.
Eight short stories of colonialism, corruption and injustice.

452 **Chansons païennes.** (Pagan songs.)
Jean-Baptiste Tiemele.   Paris: Oswald, 1969. 46p.
Poetry in French on Congolese themes.

453 **An anthology of African and Malagasy poetry in French.**
Edited by Clive Wake.   London: Oxford University Press, 1965. 181p.
This compilation in English presents some works of Martial Sinda and G. F. Tchicaya
U Tam'si. The collection is supplemented by biographical notes and an index of first
lines.

454 **Les proverbes anciens du Bas-Congo.** (The old proverbs of the lower
Congo.)
Robert L. Wannyn.   Brussels: Éditions du Vieux Planquesaule, 1983-
88. 2 vols.
This illustrated collection of proverbs and other examples of Congolese wit and
eloquence is presented in French and Kikongo.

Le Mois en Afrique. (The month in Africa.)
See item no. 525.

Art, Music and Architecture

455 African art and Oceanic art.
Edited by Francesco Abbate. London, New York: Octopus, 1972. 158p.

The sculpture and mask-making of the Fang, Bakwele, Bakota, Balumbo, Bateke and Bakongo are surveyed in short paragraphs and illustrated with a number of colour photographs.

456 African stone sculpture.
Philip Allison. London: Lund Humphries, 1968. 71p.

This short but well-illustrated guide offers some material on stone sculpture in the Congo.

457 So-called Kuyu carvings.
Anne-Marie Benezech. *African Arts*, vol. 22, no. 6 (Nov. 1988), p. 52-60.

This illustrated article analyses the variety of wooden figurines found in the Congo.

458 Art in Africa.
Tibor Bodrogi. Budapest: Kossuth, 1968. 131p. maps.

Bodrogi's survey of African art is a photographic essay containing 191 illustrations.

459 The music of central Africa.
Rose Brandel. The Hague: Nijhoff, 1961. 272p.

Described as 'an ethnomusicological study of French Equatorial Africa, the Belgian Congo, Ruanda-Urundi, Uganda and Tanganyika', this work includes material on the various ethnic groups of the Congo, as well as a bibliography and musical scores.

460 **Art of Africa: treasures from the Congo.**
    Joseph Cornet.   London: Phaidon, 1971. 365p. bibliog.

This well-illustrated work on art along the Congo concentrates on Zaïre, but contains much on the Congo as well. It is a translation by Barbara Thompson of Cornet's *Art de l'Afrique Noire au Pays du Fleuve Zaïre*. An extensive and useful bibliography appears on pages 331 to 354.

461 **The art and peoples of black Africa.**
    Jacqueline Delange.   New York: Dutton, 1974. 354p. bibliog.

Originally published in French in 1967, this English-language edition of Delange's comprehensive study of black African art includes a chapter on the western Congo basin complete with a number of monochrome illustrations connected with either the Congo or with ethnic groups found in the Congo. An excellent bibliography divided by region is also included.

462 **Musique Kongo: Babembe, Bakongo, Nseke, Balari.** (Kongo music:
    Babembe, Bakongo, Nseke, Balari.)
    Charles Duvelle (producer).   Ocora (Paris) no. OCR 35k, 1967. One
    LP record with extensive annotations included.

This is the best recording of Bakongo music ever produced.

463 **Sculpture of Africa.**
    W. Fagg, illustrated by B. Quint.   New York: Thames & Hudson,
    1958. 256p. bibliog.

Prefaced by R. Linton, this illustrated survey of African sculpture with 405 photographs includes examples of Bakongo, Bateke and Fang sculpture.

464 **African tribal sculpture: volume II, the Congo Basin tribes.**
    William Fagg.   New York: Tudor; London: Methuen, 1966. 2 vols.

More specific than the above, but also more difficult to find, this extensive work is the best in the field of traditional Congolese sculpture.

465 **The art of central Africa: tribal masks and sculpture.**
    William Fagg.   New York: New American Library, 1967. 24p.

A good brief summary of Congolese art is provided by this monograph with thirty-two colour illustrations.

466 **Fang architectonics.**
    James W. Fernandez.   Philadelphia, Pennsylvania: Institute for the
    Study of Human Issues, 1977. 41p.

Accompanied by drawings and other illustrations, this is only major work on Fang architecture.

467 **Music from an equatorial microcosm: Fang Bwiti music (with Mbiri selections).**
Recorded and annotated by James W. Fernandez. Folkways Records (New York) FE 4214. One LP record.
A selection of the Bwiti and Mbiri (Bieri) music of the Fang is presented on this recording.

468 **Notes sur la musique des Bochiman comparée à celle des Pygmees Babinga.** (Notes on the music of the Bushmen compared to that of the Babinga pygmies.)
Yvette Grimaud. Paris: Musée de l'Homme, 1957. 20p.
This interesting work in French and English compares the music of Namibia's bushmen with that of the Congo's pygmies.

469 **Congo, Gabon, Cameroun, Dahomey, Togo, illustrations.**
Andre Herviault. Paris: Peyronnet, 1930. 8p. 40 plates in portfolio.
Only 325 copies of this excellent portfolio of illustrations of French colonies were ever printed. The brief guide accompanying the collection is prefaced by Leon Petre.

470 **Les Graveurs de Poto-Poto.** (The engravers of Poto-Poto.)
Rolf Italiaaner. *Journal de la Société des Africanistes* (Paris), vol. 30, no. 2 (1960), p. 229-31.
Noting the decline of traditional Congolese art following the Second World War, French painter Pierre Lods opened an artists' school in 1951 in Poto-Poto, a poor district of Brazzaville. Drawing on almost every ethnic group in the country, this institution led a revival of African painting, drawing and design. This article describes and illustrates the work of engravers at the school.

471 **Note sur les instruments de musique Congolaise.** (Note on Congolese musical instruments).
J. N. Maquet. Brussels:Académie Royale des Sciences Coloniales, 1956. 71p. bibliog.
Accompanied by musical notations, this French-language monograph is a good introduction to the musical instruments of the Congo and Zaïre.

472 **Un mvet: chant épique Fang.** (The Mvet: a Fang epic song.)
Zwé Nguema. Paris: Armand Colin, 1972. 473p. & three 45rpm records.
This book and recording collection is the best presentation of Fang music ever produced.

473 **L'art Kota-Mahongwe: les figures funéraires du Bassin de l'Ivindo.**
(Kota-Mahongwe art: funerary figures of the Ivindo basin.)
Louis Perrois. *Arts d'Afrique Noire*, vol. 20 (1976), p. 15-37.

This article on Bakota funerary figures in Gabon is relevant to Bakota art in the Congo.

474 **The new Grove's dictionary of music.**
Edited by Stanley Sadie. London: Macmillan, vol. 4, p. 659-61.
bibliog.

Under the entries 'Congo, Republic of' and 'Congolese music', a good survey of the country's music is provided along with information on the connections between the music of the Congo River region and American jazz. Good bibliographical notes are supplied with each entry.

475 **Bakota funerary art figures.**
Ladislav Segy. *Zaïre*, vol. 6, no. 5 (May 1952), p. 451-60.

An early look at the Bakota funerary figures mentioned in item no. 473.

476 **Art history in Africa.**
Jan Vansina. London: Longman, 1984. 233p. bibliog.

Vansina's illustrated presentation of African art also includes a discussion of methodology in African art history, a subject on which he is a renowned expert. As a scholar of ethnology and history on the Congo basin's peoples, Vansina has included much on the Congo in this work, which contains a good bibliography.

Cahiers d'études Africaines. (African studies notes.)
See item no. 516.

Encyclopédie coloniale et maritime, volume V. (Colonial and maritime encyclopedia, volume five.)
See item no. 519.

Mass Media

477 Africa Confidential.
London: Miramoor, 15 Jan. 1960-. fortnightly.

This fortnightly newsletter has published excellent research on the background and details behind African political news. Material pertaining to the Congo appears on average in a dozen issues a year and is usually of a unique nature.

478 Africa Report.
New York: African-American Institute, July 1956-. monthly.

As the African-American Institute's magazine, this monthly has presented African affairs in a consistently readable manner since the first sub-Saharan nations gained their independence from European colonial powers. Issues which have appeared around important events in the Congo. These have included material on the Congo in 'Press and Radio in Africa', vol. 9, no. 2, (Feb. 1964), p. 32; Mohammed Bahri and Philippe Decraene's 'View of Congo-Brazzaville', vol. 10, no. 9, (Oct. 1965), p. 35-7; W. H. Friedland's 'Paradoxes of African Trade Unionism: Organizational Chaos and Political Potential', vol. 10, no. 5, (June 1965); A. H. House's 'Brazzaville: Revolution or Rhetoric?', vol. 16, no. 4, (April 1971). Some of the most recent major articles have been on political reform in the Congo, vol. 36, no. 1, (Jan.-Feb. 1991) and vol. 36, no. 4, (July-Aug. 1991).

479 AfricAsia.
Paris: Société d'Éditions Afrique, Asie, Amerique Latine, monthly.

The major articles on the Congo in this French magazine of Third World affairs have been 'Congo: echec à la contre-révolution' (Congo: defeat to the counter-revolution), (12 April 1970); A. Baba Miske's 'Brazzaville: il faut armer le peuple' (Brazzaville: it is necessary to arm the people), (3 & 10 May 1970) and 'Brazzaville: sept ans après les "Trois Glorieuses" ' (Brazzaville: seven years after the 'Trois Glorieuses'), (30 Aug. 1970).

480 **Afrique nouvelle.** (New Africa.)
     Dakar: 1943-. weekly.

Except for a brief period of suspension in 1972, this Senegalese weekly has provided regular news of events in the Congo and other Francophone African nations. The principal articles of the past include J. A. Makosso's 'Une Révolution qui tourne mal' (The revolution that turned bad) (6 Jan. 1965); Père Gross' 'Comment vivent nos futurs prêtres au Congo-Brazzaville?' (How alive are our priests' futures in the Congo-Brazzaville?) (2 & 29 March and 5 & 12 April 1967); S. Kiba's 'Le Congo-Brazzaville est toujours en proie à ses difficultés politiques' (The Congo-Brazzaville is always prey to political difficulties) (5 Nov. 1969); H. Latour's 'L'Avenir du Congo-Brazzaville' (The future of the Congo-Brazzaville) (23 Dec. 1970) and J. K. Sane's 'Congo: primauté au parti' (Congo: primacy of the party) (8-14 Jan. 1975).

481 **Brazzaville à l'heure de la télévision Congolaise.** (Brazzaville from the time of Congolese television.)
     Manga Bekombo.   *Revue Française de Sociologie* (Paris), vol. 7, no. 2 (April-June 1966), p. 188-99.

This short article provides a rare and interesting look at television and its effects in the Third World in general and the Congo in particular.

482 **Bulletin Quotidien de l'ACI.** (Daily bulletin of the ACI.)
     Brazzaville: Agence Congolaise d'Information, 1961-. daily.

This is the daily news bulletin of the Congolese Information Agency. Highly politicized and strongly biased in favour of the government, some of the more useful releases include pieces on labour statistics (5 May 1966); new labour union and political training for workers (6 Dec. 1966); government encouragement of agricultural vocations (26 April 1967); judicial and civil service reforms (16 Feb. 1968); a new cement plant (27 March 1968); EEC road construction financing (21 March 1968); professional training in the Congo (31 July 1968); projected 1969 government expenditure (3 Jan. 1969); and regulations of the National Council of the Revolution [CNR] (12 Aug. 1969.) As the monopoly which controls all news which Congolese and foreign journalists are allowed to print, the Agence Congolaise d'Information has had a major impact on the country's media. It is not surprising that numerous publications have rapidly come and gone due to lack of funds, lack of interest and the atmosphere of surveillance which has pervaded the country since independence. These publications have included political party organs such as the Force Ouvrière's *Conscience Ouvrière*, the MSA's *L'Essor*, the PPC's *L'AEF Nouvelle*, the UJC's *L'Eveil* and several UDDIA periodicals, *France Equateur*, *Cette Semaine AEF*, *Le Progrès* and *L'Homme Nouveau*. Other publications which have either ceased publication or become irregular are the quarterly *Bakento Ya Congo*; the monthly *Combattant Rouge* (Red fighter); the monthly *Congo-Magazine*; the monthly *Effort*; the weekly *Jeunesse et Révolution* (Youth and revolution); the weekly *Paris-Brazzaville*; the weekly sports publication *Le Stade* (The stadium); the bimonthly *Voix de la Classe Ouvrière* (Voice of the working class, which is also called *Voco*); *La Voix de la Révolution*; and *L'Eveil Congolais*.

483 **Le Courrier d'Afrique.** (The African Mail.)
     Brazzaville: 1968-82. daily.

This newspaper was, along with *Le Petit Journal de Brazzaville*, the major source of daily news in the country until it ceased publication in 1982.

484 **Dipanda.** (Independence.)
Brazzaville: JMNR, 1964-8. weekly.

This radical left-wing youth weekly contained articles reporting on Congolese governmental, political and economic news and included material on resolutions adopted by MNR central committee (2 April 1966. p. 1 & 4-5); the role of the Congolese People's Army (16 April 1966. p. 5-6); and articles by Bernard Kombo on the MNR's plans for 'carrying out the fight for national liberation', which appeared in a number of issues throughout August and September 1965. Joseph van den Reysen discussed the role of intellectuals in an avant garde party in two issues (11 & 18 July 1964.) Building an independent national economy was the subject of an article series (24 & 31 July & 7 August 1965) and Communist Chinese aid is described in the 19 March 1967 issue.

485 **Etumba.** (Star.)
Brazzaville: MNR, then PCT, 1965-. weekly.

This publication was an official organ of two successive ruling parties in the Congo. Past articles have included sociological and demographic information by Pierre Vennetier in vol. 2 (12 May 1966, p. 1, 5-6) and information on public-private industrial co-operation (1 June 1967); demands for the reorganization of state budget (7 Dec. 1967, p. 1, 11-12); the opening of a parliamentary session and speeches (23 May 1968. p. 1-2, 7); the Congolese women's union (14 Sept. 1968); a Communist Chinese-aided textile mill (20 March 1967, 26 Oct. 1968); motions carried by sugar-workers' union congress (8 July 1971. p. 1 & 3); and Congolese educational diplomas (4 Oct. 1969).

486 **L'Eveil de Pointe-Noire.** (The alert of Pointe-Noire.)
Pointe-Noire, Congo: 1959-70. daily.

L'Eveil de Pointe-Noire was the newspaper of the Congo's port city. This publication along with the low-circulation northern paper *L'Eveil de la Sangha*, the only press outside of Brazzaville, were ordered by the government to cease publication in 1970.

487 **Le Figaro.**
Paris: 1866-. daily.

In addition to regular news features on the Congo, the following are two noteworthy articles on the Congo which have appeared in this French daily newspaper: J. F. Chauvel on 'The Congolese Revolution' (6 & 7 May 1965) and D. Garric's 'Le "Coup d'Etat pour Rien" de Brazzaville' ('Brazzaville's coup for nothing'), (10-11 Aug. 1968).

488 **Index on Censorship.**
London: PEN International, monthly.

PEN International is a human rights organization for writers and journalists. This is their monthly magazine which frequently contains news about censorship and other human rights violations in the Congo, where heavy censorship was in force from 1972 to 1980 and periodically since that time.

489 **Jeune Afrique.** (Young Africa.)
Paris: 1961-. monthly.

Some important past articles on the Congo from this left-wing French magazine of African affairs are 'Premier "musée imaginaire" de l'Afrique noire' (Black Africa's first imaginary museum) by Michel Leiris (21 May 1967); 'Une Révolution dans tous les domaines' (A revolution in all spheres) by Jean Rous (9 July 1967); 'L'Heure du ciment' (The time of cement) (22 April 1968); 'An V de la révolution' (Year five of the revolution) (28 July 1968); and 'Quel socialisme à Brazzaville?' (10 March 1970). July 1968 also saw the publication of several supplements by Jeune Afrique on agriculture, animal production, banking, forestry and industry and mining, all of which included information on the Congo. Also for this period are some anonymous articles on examination results (22 July 1968); potash industry (5 May 1969); and student protests (12 May 1969). In the early 1970s S. Diallo wrote a number of articles on the Congo: 'Congo: entre révolutionnaires' (11 March 1972); 'Zaïre-Congo: la dernière réconciliation?' (Zaïre-Congo: the last reconciliation?) (30 Sept. 1972); 'Congo: la contradiction principale' (Congo: the principal contradiction) (7 Oct. 1972); and 'Le Complot de Brazzaville' (The Brazzaville plot) (10 March 1973). Important recent articles are 'Congo 73' by B. Crimi (11 August 1973); 'La Phase démocratique et populaire' (The democratic and popular phase) (Supplement A, 28 Dec. 1974); 'Henri Lopès, un ecrivain fourvoyé dans la politique' (Henri Lopès, a misled writer in politics) by S. Kamara (5 May 1982); and 'Congo 82' by S. Gharbi (11 August 1982).

490 **Journal Officiel de la Republique du Congo.** (Official journal of the Republic of the Congo.)
Brazzaville: Congolese government, 1958-. fortnightly.

Articles in this official organ of the Congolese government have tended to display extreme biases in favour of government policies. Three important early examples are pieces on the Congolese labour code (9 July 1964); a decree on workers' leave (15 Feb. 1966); and decrees establishing military units and cadres within them (1 March 1966).

491 **Le Monde.** (The world.)
Paris: 19 Dec. 1944-. daily except Monday.

Important past articles on the Congo in this authoritative French newspaper are J. Nere's 'Promesses et faiblesses du Congo-Brazzaville' (Promises and weaknesses of the Congo-Brazzaville) (31 Dec. 1966 & 12 Jan. 1967); P. Decraene's 'Confusion et désarroi' (Confusion and disarray) (11 Nov. 1969); Gilbert Comte wrote a serialized article on the Congolese revolution (Paris) (25, 26 & 27 March 1970); P. J. Franceschini's 'Le Congo de la "radicalisation" ' (The Congo of 'radicalization') (21, 22 & 23 March 1976); and 'Congo 1981: le Marxisme en question' (Congo 1981: Marxism in question) (31 Dec. 1981 & 2 Jan. 1982). An article on the Congolese revolution also appeared in the 25 April 1967 and 3 May 1967 issues.

492 **Le Monde diplomatique.** (The diplomatic world.)
Paris: May 1954-. monthly

Le Monde's magazine of foreign affairs has featured a number of articles on the Congo, including Gilbert Comte's 'Une république populaire sous les tropiques' (A People's Reublic in the tropics) (May 1970); J. Teillac & H. Robert's 'Le Congo: est-il socialiste?' (The Congo: is it socialist?) (April 1973); and T. Lamaury's 'Congo: le socialisme n'est pas un jeu de mots' (Congo: socialism is not a play on words) (Feb. 1974).

493   **Mweti.** (Star.)
Brazzaville: 1977-. three times weekly.
Currently this paper is the Congo's principal source of national and international news.

494   **Le Petit Journal de Brazzaville.** (Little Brazzaville Journal.)
Brazzaville: 1960-82. daily.
Also called *Le Journal de Brazzaville* (The Brazzaville Journal), this newspaper was, along with *Le Courrier d'Afrique*, the major source of daily news in the country until their disappearance in 1982.

495   **La Semaine.** (The Week.)
Brazzaville: Archdiocese of Brazzaville, 1952-. weekly.
Originally *La Semaine de l'Afrique Française Equatoriale* (The French Equatorial African Week), then *La Semaine Africaine* (The African Week), this Roman Catholic weekly also circulates in Gabon, Chad and the Central African Republic. It has survived the gauntlet of government censorship over the years by avoiding the political. As *Le Semaine Africaine*, it published L. Badila's 'Mythes et réalités au Congo-Brazzaville' (Myths and realities in the Congo-Brazzaville) (15 Dec. 1963) and 'La révolution violée' (The violated revolution) (12 Nov. 1964.) However, after the final change of title in 1965 its articles stuck to such subjects as glass and paper industries (10 October 1965, 18 March 1968); preliminary work on the Kouilou dam (17 April 1966); rural education (19 June 1966); a handicrafts co-operative (22 May 1966); Congolese budgets (25 Dec. 1966 & 1 Jan. 1967); radio and television broadcasting (June 1967); Kouilou potash deposits (6 August 1967); administrative reorganization (10 Sept. 1967); a cement plant (31 March 1968); the Makabana mining school (28 April 1968); a North Korean-aided match factory (27 Oct. 1968) and the UDEAC (27 Oct. 1968).

496   **West Africa.**
London: West Africa, 1917-. weekly.
One of a few English-language publications which has regular news items on the Congo. Some of its best early articles on the Congo include 'The coup that wasn't' (10 Aug. 1965); 'Brazzaville: ten years of revolution' (13 & 20 Aug. 1973); 'Who killed Ngouabi?' (28 March 1977); and 'Brazzaville tightrope' (4 April 1977.) More recent articles are 'Congo: Oil or Nothing' (26 Sept. 1988) on the oil price slump; 'Congo: Closed Friendship' (12 Dec. 1988); 'Conference Conundrum: Strikers Hold the Reins as Democracy Comes Closer' (25 Feb. 1991); 'Year of the Conferences: Old Guard Gives in the Popular Demands' (6 Jan. 1992); 'Mauled by the Military, PM Seeks Comeback after Radio Coup' (27 Jan. 1992); 'Not Much of a Big Deal?' (17 Feb. 1992) on the disappearance of an informer on the UTA airliner bombing; 'Settling the Polemics' (4 May 1992); 'Transition Prolonged' (25 May 1992); 'Quaint Change of Guard' (7 Sept. 1992); 'Lissouba's Worries' (7 Dec. 1992); and 'Democracy by Intimidation?' (21 Dec. 1992) for an interview with Congolese President Pascal Lissouba.

The Congo.
See item no. 521.

Biographies

497 **Personnalités publiques de l'Afrique centrale: Cameroun, RCA, Congo, Gabon, Tchad.** (Public personalities in central Africa, Cameroon, Central African Republic, Congo, Gabon, Chad.)
Anonymous. Paris: Ediafric, 1968. 373p.

This French-language biographical reference work provides information on post-independence political figures in the Congo.

498 **Brazza explorateur: l'Ogooué 1875-1879.** (Brazza explorer: the Ogooué 1875-1879.)
Henri Brunschwig. Paris, The Hague: Mouton, 1966. 215p.

Brunschwig's biography of Pierre Savorgnan de Brazza is drawn mainly from de Brazza's own letters and reports. This illustrated work covers the French explorer's early travels in Gabon and the Congo.

499 **Brazza explorateur: les traités Makoko 1880-1882.** (Brazza explorer: the Makoko treaties 1880-1882.)
Henri Brunschwig. Paris, The Hague: Mouton, 1972. 298p.

This continuation of the above item covers the period of de Brazza's establishment of French claims on the Congo.

500 **Congo explorer, Pierre Savorgnan de Brazza: 1852-1905.**
Jeanne Carbonnier.   New York: Scribner, 1960. 152p.
A short, illustrated biography of de Brazza.

501 **Félix Eboué: gouverneur et philosophe.** (Felix Eboué: governor and
philosopher.)
Elie W. Castor, Raymond Tarcy.   Paris: Éditions L'Harmattan, 1984.
359p.
This French-language book is the best biography available of French Equatorial
Africa's Second World War governor, Felix Eboué, France's first black colonial
governor. It includes twenty-four pages of illustrations and a short bibliography.

502 **Brazza et la prise de possession du Congo.** (Brazza and the acquisition
of the Congo.)
Catherine Coquery-Vidrovitch.   Paris, The Hague: Mouton, 1969.
502p.
This well-written study of the French colonization of the Congo concentrates on the
life of Pierre Savorgnan de Brazza.

503 **Les constructeurs de la France d'outre-mer.** (The builders of France
overseas.)
Edited by R. Delavignette, C. A. Julien.   Paris: Correa, 1945. 525p.
bibliog.
Pierre Savorgnan de Brazza and other important figures in the history of French
Equatorial Africa are included in this work which contains biographical notes on the
most prominent French imperialists along with extracts from their writings.
Bibliographies appear at the end of each chapter.

504 **Au Congo Français: Monseigneur Carrie, 1842-1904.** (To the French
Congo: Monsignor Carrie, 1842-1904.)
J. Delcourt.   Paris: J. Delcourt, [n.d.]. 2 vols.
This is a well-written and detailed biography of the first French Catholic missionary to
the Congo.

505 **A cardinal who spoke truth to power.**
Randall Fegley.   *The Christian Century*, vol. 104, no. 11 (8 April
1987), p. 325-6.
Activist Congolese theologian Cardinal Émile Biayenda was murdered in March 1977
during the political instability which followed the assassination of President Marien
Ngouabi. This article provides a brief biography of Biayenda, an account of his death
and a summary of his beliefs and contributions to both the Congo and the Roman
Catholic Church.

Biographies

506   John Holt: a British merchant in West Africa in the era of imperialism.
Cherry Gertzel.   unpublished thesis. Nuffield College, Oxford: 1959.

This unpublished doctoral thesis provides good biographical sketch of British trader John Holt whose company was of prime importance in opening the western equatorial coasts of Africa to European trade, and who supported calls for the investigations probing the abuses of concessionary companies in both the Belgian and French Congos.

507   La vie de Marien Ngouabi: 1938-1977. (The life of Marien Ngouabi: 1938-1977.)
Theophile Obenga.   Paris: Présence Africaine, 1977. 334p.

Written by his fellow M'Boshi tribesman, writer Theophile Obenga, this French-language biography of Ngouabi offers an uncritical look at the life of the assassinated Congolese president.

508   Félix Tchicaya: premier parlementaire Congolais (1903-1961), in memoriam. (Felix Tchicaya: first Congolese parliamentarian [1903-1961], in memoriam.)
Republic of the Congo Ministry of Information.   Brazzaville: Imprimerie Officielle, 1961. 23p.

This obituary in pamphlet form provides a good biography of Vili politician Félix Tchicaya, who was the Congo's first African representative to the French National Assembly.

509   André Matsoua: fondateur du mouvement de liberation du Congo.
(André Matswa: founder of the Congo's liberation movement.)
Martial Sinda.   Dakar, Abidjan: Nouvelles Éditions Africaines, 1977. 94p.

This short biography of André Matswa incorporates a great deal of historical material on his messianic movement and early Congolese nationalism, but its tone and style verge on that of hagiography.

510   The new Africans.
Edited by Sidney Taylor.   New York: G.P. Putnam's Sons, 1967. 504p.

Compiled from the work of fifty Reuters' correspondents, this one-volume guide to Africa's leaders in the 1960s is valuable for its hundreds of short biographies. The biographical essays are organized in alphabetical order by country and then by subject. Each country is introduced with a summary of several pages and includes a map, photographs of the country and portraits of most of the individuals discussed. Material on the Congo appears on pages 60–73. This includes a seven page introduction and biographies of E. Ebouka-Babakas, David Charles Ganao, André Hombessa, Pascal Lissouba, François-Luc Macosso, Alphonse Massemba-Debat, Aimé Matsika, Georges Mouyabi, Pierre M'Vouama, Ambroise Noumazalay and Fulbert Youlou.

511 **Paul du Chaillu: gorilla hunter.**
Michel Vaucaire. New York: Harper, 1930. 322p.
Translated from the French, this biography of Paul du Chaillu, American adventurer and explorer of equatorial Africa is interesting for its French point of view.

512 **Eboué.**
Brian Weinstein. New York: Oxford University Press, 1972. 350p.
Weinstein's excellent biography of Félix Eboué, the first black French colonial governor, is the best available in English.

513 **Brazza of the Congo.**
Richard West. Newton Abbot, England: Victorian Book Club, 1973. 304p. bibliog.
This well-written biography of Count Pierre Savorgnan de Brazza describes the life and accomplishments of its subject and goes on to provide a short history of the Congo up to the time of independence.

Two trips to gorilla land and the cataracts of the Congo.
See item no. 9.

Exploration and adventures in Equatorial Africa.
See item no. 11.

The country of the dwarfs.
See item no. 13.

A journey to Ashango-land and further penetration into equatorial Africa.
See item no. 14.

Stories of the gorilla country.
See item no. 15.

Travels in the Congo.
See item no. 18.

Trader Horn.
See item no. 19.

Conférences et lettres de Pierre Savorgnan de Brazza sur ses trois explorations dans l'Ouest Africain. (Lectures and letters of Pierre Savorgnan de Brazza on his three expeditions to the African west.)
See item no. 24.

Through the dark continent.
See item no. 26.

Congo.
See item no. 111.

Matswa.
See item no. 172.

Biographies

La passion de Simon Kimbangu. (The passion of Simon Kimbangu.)
See item no. 176.

Simon Kimbangu, prophete et martyr Zaïrois. (Simon Kimbangu, Zaïrean prophet and martyr.)
See item no. 185.

Reference Works and Scholarly Journals

514 Africa research bulletin.

Exeter, England: Jan. 1964-. monthly.

This research publication is divided into two sections: Series A, political, social and cultural; and Series B, economic, financial and technical. Over the years a good deal of material on the Congo has been regularly reported and analysed by this monthly.

515 Bulletin de l'Institut de Recherches Scientifiques au Congo. (Bulletin of the Institute for Scientific Research in the Congo.)

Brazzaville: Institut de Recherches Scientifiques au Congo, 1962-. annual.

This French language publication of scientific findings in the Congo replaced the *Bulletin de l'Institut d'Études Centrafricaines* (Bulletin of the Institute for Central African Studies) (1945-60), which in turn had replaced the *Bulletin de la Société des Recherches Congolaises* (Bulletin of the Congolese research society) (1922-39.) Among its highlights is A. Stauch's 'Contribution à l'etude de la pêche dans la cuvette Congolaise' (A Contribution to the study of the fishes of the Congo basin), vol. 2, (1963) p. 49-85. The institute also published various periodicals in specialized fields, such as *Cahiers de sciences humaines* (Human sciences notes.), which published G. Althabe's 'Etude du chomage à Brazzaville en 1957' (A study of unemployment in Brazzaville in 1957), vol. 1, no. 2, (1963) and *Cahiers d'ORSTOM* (ORSTOM notes) (1963-present), which published A. Jacquot's 'Les Langues du Congo-Brazzaville' (The languages of the Congo-Brazzaville), vol. 8, no. 4, (1971). These publications and institutions originated when the French set up the Office de la Recherche Scientifique des Territoires d'Outre-Mer (ORSTOM) in 1944 to conduct research in natural sciences, sociology, geography, linguistics, medicine and education in French colonies.

516 Cahiers d'études Africaines. (African studies notes.)

Paris: Ecole des Hautes Études en Sciences Sociales, 1960-. quarterly.

One of the most prestigious African studies journals in the Francophone world, *Cahiers d'Études Africaines* has published works on the Congo in both French and

English. Perhaps the best of these is Catherine Coquery-Vidrovitch's 'Les Idées Économiques de Brazza et les Premières Tentatives de Compagnie de Colonisation au Congo Français 1885-1898', vol. 5, no. 1 (Jan.-March 1965), p. 57-82. A Congolese anti-witchcraft movement is described in vol. 6, no. 4 (Oct.-Dec. 1966) and P. Bonnafé's 'Une Classe d'age politique, la JMNR du Congo-Brazzaville' (A political youth class, the JMNR in the Congo-Brazzaville) vol. 8, no. 3 (July-Sept. 1968) discusses the radicalization of the Congo's youth. A recent article by Bogumil Jewsiewicki offers a study of folk-painters (vol. 31, no. 123 [1991]).

517 **Cahiers d'Outre-mer.** (Overseas notes.)
   Bordeaux, France: Institut de la France d'Outre-Mer de Bordeaux, 1948-57, then Institut de Géographie de la Faculte des Lettres de Bordeaux, 1958-. quarterly.

The French language geographical review has provided numerous articles on the Congo. Early examples include Louis Papy's 'Les Populations Batéké' (The Bateke people), vol. 2 (April-June 1949), p. 112-34; Jacques Richard-Molard's 'Groupes ethniques et collectivités d'Afrique noire' (Ethnic groups and black African collectivity), vol. 5 (April-June 1952), p. 97-107; an anonymous piece entitled 'Banlieue noire de Brazzaville' (Black suburbs of Brazzaville), vol. 10 (June 1957), p. 131-57; Alain Auger's 'Notes sur les centres urbains secondaires du Congo' (Notes on the secondary urban centres of the Congo), vol. 21 (Jan.-March 1968), p. 29-55; Pierre Vennetier's 'La Vie agricole urbaine à Pointe-Noire' (Urban agricultural life in Pointe-Noire), vol. 14 (March 1961); 'Population et économie du Congo-Brazzaville' (The population and economy of the Congo-Brazzaville), vol. 15 (Oct.-Dec. 1962); 'La Société Industrielle et Agricole du Niari (SIAN)' (The Niari Industrial and Agricultural Company [SIAN]), vol. 16 (Jan.-March 1963); 'l'Urbanisation et ses conséquences au Congo-Brazzaville' (Urbanization and its consequence in the Congo-Brazzaville), vol. 16 (July-Sept. 1963), p. 263-80; and 'Les ports du Gabon et du Congo-Brazzaville' (The ports of Gabon and the Congo-Brazzaville), vol. 22 (Oct.-Dec. 1969), p. 337-55. Other articles include pieces on SIAN (Jan.-March 1965); and western and central African demography by Bernard Kayser (Jan.-March 1965).

518 **Chroniques d'Outre-Mer.** (Overseas chronicles.)
   Paris: Ministry of Overseas France, 1951-8. ten per annum.

This official periodical of the French government provides much information on the transformation of the colonies of the French Empire to independent nations within the French Community in the 1950s.

519 **Encyclopédie coloniale et maritime, volume V.** (Colonial and maritime encyclopedia, volume five.)
   Edited by Eugène Guernier.   Paris: Éditions Coloniales et Maritimes, 1950. 590p. maps. bibliog.

Volume Five of this detailed and useful colonial era reference work is devoted to French Equatorial Africa. Much information is provided on French activity in the colony and the Congo's geography, history, cultures and economy. Especially good is Jean-Hilaire Aubame's chapter 'La Conférence de Brazzaville' (p. 183-6.) Illustrations, maps, music and a bibliography are included.

520 **Encyclopédie mensuelle d'outre-mer.** (The monthly overseas encyclopaedia.)
Paris: 1950-1967. monthly.

This French monthly published several lengthy works on the Congo including Georges Balandier's 'Messianisme des Ba-Kongo' (Bakongo messianism) (Aug. 1951); J. Pargoire's 'La Vallée du Niari' (The Niari valley) (Jan. 1955); and R. Frey's 'Brazzaville' (Aug.-Sept. 1964).

521 **The Congo.**
David Hilling, Robert Cornevin, Edith Hodgkinson.   In: *Africa South of the Sahara.* London: Europa, 1970-. annual. bibliog.

Entries in this authoritative annual are divided into a number of sections beginning with essays on physical and social geography, recent history and the economy. These sections are written by leading experts on the particular country covered. Following these background pieces are a survey of area, population, economics, transport and education statistics and a directory which describes the country's constitution, government, legislature, political organizations, diplomatic representation, courts, religious institution, the mass media, finance, trade and industry and transport. This data is accompanied by appropriate names and addresses. Each entry ends with a short bibliography.

522 **Keesing's contemporary archives.**
London: Longman, 1954-. monthly.

Keesing's researchers compile regular records of political, diplomatic and economic events throughout the world. These compilations, which provide an excellent base for research, are gleaned from several hundred sources in the world press and provide an ongoing archive of significant events, personalities in power, cabinet compositions, election results and other facts and figures for all countries. Renamed *Keesing's Record of World Events* after 1988, its coverage of the Congo and also the Franc Zone and its component organizations (as separate entries) has been exceptionally thorough but news items have often been delayed for considerable lengths of time. In many ways Keesing's has presented and continues to present one of the most comprehensive, accurate and objective accounts in English of events in the Congo.

523 **Encyclopedia of the Third World.**
Edited by George Thomas Kurian.   New York, Oxford: Facts on File, 1992. 3 vols.

This general reference on the Third World is amazingly thorough in its treatment of the Congo on pages 427 to 444. In addition to basic facts and figures, short sections are provided on the Congo's geographical features, climate, population, ethnic composition, languages, religions, history, constitution, government, human rights, local government, foreign policy, parliament, political parties, the economy, public finance, currency, banking, agriculture, manufacturing, mining, energy, labour, commerce, transport, communications, defence, education, legal system, law enforcement, health, nutrition, media, culture and social welfare. A useful glossary, chronology and a short bibliography are included.

524 Africa contemporary record.
Edited by Colin Legum. London: Rex Collings; New York: Africana, 1969-. annual.

The Congo entries of this vast annual (1969 to the present) provide a continuous record of events, personalities, policies and issues relating to the country.

525 Le Mois en Afrique. (The month in Africa.)
Dakar: 1966-80, Paris: 1980-. monthly.

Also known as the *Revue Française d'Etude Politiques Africaines*. (The French review of African political studies), this monthly has provided a wealth of articles on the Congo in a number of subjects. Major articles have included 'Le Mystère s'epaissit' (The mystery thickens), (Sept. 1966); L. V. Thomas' 'Le Socialisme Congolais' (Congolese socialism), (Nov. 1966); Pierre Biarnès' 'Congo-Brazzaville: un coup de Barre à droite' (Congo-Brazzaville: Barre's coup to the right), (Feb. 1968); P. L. Prévost's 'L'Union Douanière et Economique de l'Afrique Central (UDEAC)' (Oct. 1968); the anonymous 'Une Révolution inquiète et permanente' (An anxious and lasting revolution), (Dec. 1969); D. Renaud's 'Difficultés economiques et tensions politiques' (Economic difficulties and political tensions), (Feb. 1970); Gilbert Comte's 'Echec aux "conservateurs" ' (Defeat of the 'conservatives'), (April 1970) and 'L'Embarras Français' (French embarrassment), (June 1970); and P. Decraene's 'Huit années d'histoire Congolaise' (Eight years of Congolese history), (Dec. 1974.); O. Postel-Viney's 'La Socialisme à petits pas' (Socialism slowly), (27, 28 & 30 April 1975); D. Desjeux's 'Le Congo est-il situationiste?: vingt ans d'histoire politique de la classe dirigeante Congolaise' (Twenty years of Congolese elite political history), (Oct.-Nov. 1980); and S. Crapuchet's 'Femmes villageoises des Plateaux du Congo' (Village women in the Plateaux region of the Congo), (March-April 1982). Several important articles by G. Danino also discuss Congolese literature: 'L'Image de la femme dans la littérature Congolaise' (The female image in Congolese literature), (Aug.-Sept. 1981); 'La Notion d'identité dans la littérature Congolaise' (The notion of identity in Congolese literature), (April-May 1983) and 'La Prise de conscience du racisme colonial à travers la littérature Congolaise d'expression Française' (The grip of colonial racist perception on Francophone Congolese literature), (April-May 1981).

526 A historical dictionary of the People's Republic of the Congo.
Virginia Thompson, Richard Adloff. Metuchen, New Jersey: Scarecrow, 1984. 239p. bibliog.

This reference work on the Congo is useful and contains much information not found elsewhere in English, but due to its format hardly displays the careful scholarship of Thompson and Adloff's other work. Although described as a historical dictionary, this book contains a large amount of geographical, biographical and economic data and a bibliography. This work is very strong on Congolese political history and political biography since the Second World War. However, the coverage of all periods before the 20th century is weak and also on the important cultural and religious aspects of the country's history. Photographs of the Congo's presidents appear with their individual entries.

Area handbook for the People's Republic of the Congo (Congo Brazzaville).
See item no. 3.

Bibliographies

527 **Politics and government in former French West and Equatorial Africa: a critical bibliography.**
J. A. Ballard. *Journal of Modern African Studies*, vol. 3, no. 3/4 (Dec. 1965), p. 589-605.

This bibliographical essay is a good beginning for anyone researching the politics of the Congo.

528 **Bibliographie de l'Afrique Equatoriale Française.** (A bibliography of French Equatorial Africa.)
Georges Bruel.   Paris: Larose, 1914. 326p.

This early bibliography of French Equatorial Africa provides much information on rare early works in French.

529 **Materials on west African history in French archives.**
Patricia Carson.   London: Athlone, 1963. 170p.

This bibliography of French sources contains numerous entries on western equatorial Africa, including the Congo.

530 **Guide bibliographique sommaire d'histoire militaire et coloniale Françaises.** (A concise bibliographic guide to French military and colonial history.)
Edited by René Couret.   Paris: Imprimerie Nationale, 1969. 522p.

Numerous French-language sources related to French colonialism in the Congo are found in this large well-organized bibliography.

Bibliographies

531 **Education in the states of equatorial Africa: a bibliographical essay.**
David E. Gardinier. *Africana Journal*, vol. 3, no. 3 (1972), p. 7-20.
Focusing on education, this bibliographical essay provides both colonial and post-colonial sources.

532 **Bibliographie d'histoire coloniale, 1900-1930, Belgique.** (A bibliography of colonial history, 1900-1930 – Belgium.)
Michel Huisman, Paul Jacquet. Paris: Société de l'Histoire des Colonies Françaises, 1932. 81p.
This useful bibliography contains mainly official Belgian sources, some of which offer information on the French Congo and relations between the two Congos and their colonial masters.

533 **Sources d'information sur l'Afrique noire Francophone et Madagascar.**
(Information sources on Francophone black Africa and Madagascar.)
Laurence Porges. Paris: Ministéré de la Co-operation, 1988. 389p.
The best of the most recent French-language bibliographies related to the Congo.

534 **Official publications of French Equatorial Africa, French Cameroons and Togo, 1946-1958.**
Julian W. Witherell. Washington, DC: Library of Congress, 1964. 78p.
Scholars pursuing studies in Congolese colonial history and politics will find this short work essential in locating post-Second World War official French sources.

535 **French-speaking central Africa: a guide to official publications in American libraries.**
Julian W. Witherell. Washington, DC: Library of Congress, 1973. 314p.
This excellent bibliographical reference deals mainly with official or officially-sponsored publications, articles and translations, from the colonial era and the immediate post-independence period. This bibliography contains seventy-two specific entries on the Congo as well as more general material which includes the Congo.

536 **The United States and Africa: a guide to U.S. official documents and government sponsored publications 1785-1975.**
Julian W. Witherell. Washington, DC: Library of Congress, 1978. 949p.
This large, general bibliography contains some sources on the history of US-Congolese relations.

Index

The index is a single alphabetical sequence of authors (personal and corporate), titles of publications and subjects. Index entries refer both to the main items and to other works mentioned in the notes to each item. Title entries are in italics. Numeration refers to individual items.

159

Map of Congo

This map shows the more important towns and other features.

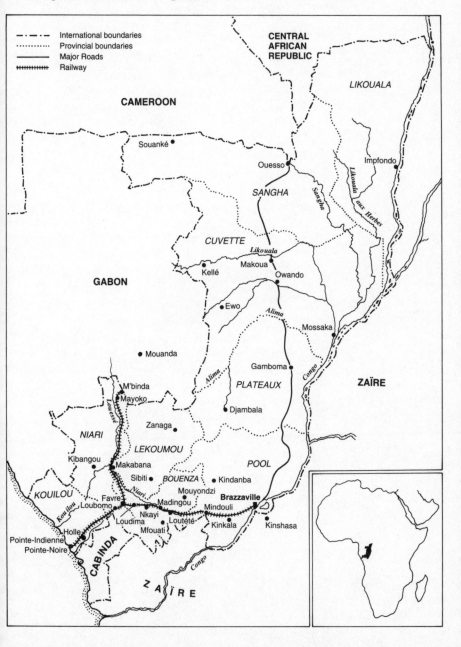